World University Library

The World University Library is an international series
of books, each of which has been specially commissioned.
The authors are leading scientists and scholars from all over
the world who, in an age of increasing specialisation, see the
need for a broad, up-to-date presentation of their subject.
The aim is to provide authoritative introductory books for
university students which will be of interest also to the general
reader. Publication of the series takes place in Britain,
France, Germany, Holland, Italy. Spain, Sweden and
the United States.

Frontispiece: The Dutch Republic at the end of the Thirty Years
War (including southern territory ratified by the treaties of 1648).

FRIESLAND
□ Franeker

GRONINGEN
Groningen

HOLLAND

Medemblik
Enkhuizen
Alkmaar
Hoorn
Purmurend
Edam
Monnikendam
Haarlem
Amsterdam

OVERIJSSEL

Harderwyk

UTRECHT
□ Utrecht

GELDERLAND

Leyden
Delft
Gouda
R.Lek
Schiedam
Schoonhoven
Rotterdam
R.Waal
The Brill
Gorinchem
Dordrecht

ZEELAND
LANDS OF THE ESTATES GENERAL

R.Maas

● Towns with a vote in the Provincial States assembly
□ University towns

Charles Wilson

The Dutch Republic

and the civilisation of the seventeenth century

World University Library

McGraw-Hill Book Company
New York Toronto

Library of Congress Catalog Card Number: 68-14342
Phototypeset by BAS Printers Limited, Wallop, Hampshire, England
Printed by Officine Grafiche Arnoldo Mondadori, Verona, Italy

Contents

List of Maps

1 Political and cultural origins of the Republic

When the Emperor Charles v abdicated in 1555, he handed over to his son, Philip the Second of Spain, his Netherlands possessions. In all these comprised seventeen provinces. Three of them were provinces which Charles himself had acquired in his lifetime. The other fourteen he had inherited from his predecessors, the dukes of Burgundy. They stretched from the Frisian islands in the north to the borders of France in the south; from the western seaboard of the European continent in the west to the borders of Germany in the east. Broadly speaking they covered the present-day area of Benelux, together with what later became a strip of northern France and they were one of the two richest, most industrious, densely peopled and highly urbanised areas of the mid sixteenth century world. The other – north Italy – was past its prime. Neither its economy nor its culture any longer had the buoyancy and vitality that characterised the Netherlands.

This was the heart of the Holy Roman Empire of Charles v. Here, at Ghent, he was born. From here came many of his counsellors. More important still, this was the major source of the wealth and credit by which his government and his wars were sustained. Yet within a few years of a solemn abdication which took place amidst moving scenes of general grief, the entire Netherlands were in revolt against his heir and against Spanish rule. A quarter of a century later still, the northern provinces – especially Holland and Zeeland – were well on the way to breaking loose from the southern provinces. Half a century later, at the Truce of 1609 between Spain and the northern provinces, this break was an accomplished fact, legally ratified by the great treaties of 1648 that ended the Thirty Years War. The Burgundian-Habsburg kingdom of the Low Countries had disappeared, giving place to two separate states – the independent Dutch Republic in the north and the Spanish Netherlands, still obedient to Spain, in the south. From these have emerged the present day states of the Netherlands (commonly known as Holland) and of Belgium.

The twists and turns, triumphs and catastrophes of this Eighty Years War compose one of the most dramatic, bloody, and confused episodes of early modern European history. Yet it was not merely senseless or destructive, as the wars had been that had recently ravaged north Italy. On the contrary, it was to inaugurate a new concept of national political organisation in Europe. It provokes two major questions. Why did the Netherlands as a whole rebel against Spain? And why did only the seven northern provinces survive to achieve independence?

The orthodox answer to the first question which was given until comparatively recently was that the revolt was part of the manifest destiny of a people propelled by an irresistible urge to freedom, independence and Protestantism. They were accordingly roused to rebellion against a foreign, popish government intent on introducing the Inquisition and suppressing liberty with Spanish arms and troops. This simple formula no longer satisfies. Recent students of the revolt have stressed that it was not a single movement; it was a *congeries* of revolts by different classes and groups with many, often conflicting motives. In its early phases it represented predominantly the resistance of the feudal magnates (mainly Catholics) against the attempts of Philip to modernise, centralise and bureaucratise the loose and medieval forms of government that he found operating in his new dominions. For whereas in France, England, and Spain the 'state' was beginning to appear in a recognisably modern form, the Netherlands remained medieval, politically and administratively atomised. Nowhere was the overmighty subject so unbiddable, the burgher richer or more obstinate, nor the prince more hard up. At every turn, Philip found himself faced by a complex protective tangle of traditional 'liberties', noble, ecclesiastical, municipal, that seemed cunningly contrived to defeat the process of 'government' and reform. Philip was determined to suppress these

obstacles, to enhance his limited overlordship over these rich but unruly provinces, to be a real king, to rule.

At this stage, then, leadership of the revolt came from the nobility, even from the bishops and abbots. In the late 1560s, it was Count Egmont, Count Horne and William, Prince of Orange (all as yet Catholics) who were the symbols of resistance to Spanish governors and troops, to the Inquisition and the reorganisation of the Netherlands Church. Yet swiftly the rebellion spread and diversified. Everywhere, but most fiercely in the textile manufacturing districts of Flanders, the Calvinist movement was gathering force. Here again, the Protestant strength was greater – as yet – in the south than in the north. Ghent was long to remain one of its most turbulent centres. The main weight of the ferocious vengeance loosed by Philip's Spanish military commander, the Duke of Alba, was directed against the heretics. But the measures he took had the effect of stirring up the latent opposition of another powerful section of the Netherlands people: the merchant class of the

GRONINGE

GRONIN

FRIESLAND

DRENTHE

OVERIJSSEL

R.Ijssel

HOLLAND

• Amsterdam

Utrecht

• The Hague

UTRECHT

• Rotterdam

R.Lek

GELDERLAND

R.Waal

R.Rhine

ZEELAND

BRABANT

GELDER
LAND

• Antwerp

R.Scheldt

FLANDERS

MECHLIN

LIMBURG

• Brussels

R.Maas

ARTOIS

HAINAULT

NAMUR

R.Meuse

CAMBRAI

LUXEMBURG

☐ Dutch / Flemish speaking area

☐ French speaking area

towns. For the war had to be paid for, and Alba proposed to lay the burden on Netherlands trade in the shape of an excise tax, the notorious 'tenth penny'. This solidified merchant opposition to Spanish rule.

All the forces of trade and Protestantism were now united and aligned against Alba. Simultaneously, the appeal of Calvinism showed every sign of spreading (as it did in England and France too) to the lesser nobility and gentry, a discontented class hard hit by inflation and taxation. From their ranks came many of the leaders of the 'Beggars', a growing resistance group which initiated the capture of the vital western ports of the Brill and Flushing in 1572. Hence a more powerful grip by the rebels on the sea approaches to Holland and Zeeland. Meanwhile, the active rebel component of the burgher class in the towns joined with the Calvinists to withstand the siege which the Spaniards now laid, often with most bloody slaughter, to cities like Haarlem, Leyden and Alkmaar.

Another twenty years of war were to pass before the Spaniards were finally worsted in the north. In the south great cities like Antwerp, Ghent, Ypres and others lay in ruins; dykes were broken, villages deserted, the countryside devastated. The losses of both sides were enormous. The Truce of 1609, conceived as a pause for breath, was in fact the effective date from which a new, different, indeed unique state, the Dutch Republic, made its appearance in Europe. It seemed, to contemporaries, an improbable entity, less a unitary state than an alliance of seven provinces, led by the province of Holland, the most powerful and wealthy. And it had not one head but two: the Stadholder was Maurice, the son of William of Orange, but hardly less powerful was the Landsadvocaat of Holland, Oldenbarneveldt. Behind Maurice stood the Calvinist Church, its ministers and most fanatical supporters, drawn largely from the humbler strata of society:

behind Oldenbarneveldt, the wealth and power of one of the most stubborn and resourceful classes of men in the federation, the merchant rulers (or 'regents') of the Dutch cities. While the Orangists wanted to carry on the war with Spain, the regents' aim was to restore peace and increase prosperity. A large part of the 17th century in the new Republic was taken up with this quarrel.

To come back to the second question: why did the seven northern provinces emerge independent and the rest fall back into 'obedience' to Spain? It can no longer be argued that either the aristocratic or the Calvinist or burgher opposition was originally or naturally stronger in the north than in the south. On the contrary, the nobility were most strongly entrenched in the south, and were mainly French speaking (Walloon); Calvinism was probably stronger there too; and compared to the wealthy burghers of Antwerp or Ghent, the merchants of Leyden or Alkmaar were only a modestly well-to-do class. Culturally, too, the south had been the centre of the great creative movement of the late Middle Ages. Although the 'Flemish school' of painters drew some of its members from Haarlem and Gouda, its roots were in Ghent, Bruges, Brussels, Liège: its greatest masters were Jan van Eyck, Roger van der Weyden, the mystic Hieronymus Bosch – all Flemings or Brabanters – its great teaching schools at Ghent or Bruges. Art reflected and profited by the general prosperity of the southern cities. Long before the defeat and decline of the south, Flemish painting had been slowly detaching itself from its early spiritual and devotional preoccupations. As with so many phenomena often later regarded as Dutch and northern, the seeds of secular realism can be found in the representation of nature and man by the southern painters of the fifteenth century. Like men, money and ideas, art emigrated northwards. Why?

Regarding the religious or nationalist explanation as invalid, many recent historians (the great innovator being the late Professor

Geyl) have looked to geography and strategy to explain the survival and victory of the north. The Republic consisted (they have argued) simply of those provinces which could be defended against Spanish attack coming from the south. That meant those provinces which lay north of the great rivers. Rhine, Maas, Waal, Lek, and the great estuaries which ran athwart the Netherlands from east to west. These formed a natural barrier behind which a great national fortress against Spain could be built. Here resistance, especially Protestant resistance, could flourish and grow. There was nothing predestined therefore in the formation of the Dutch Republic. It was simply the consequence of war and the nature of the terrain over which that war was fought.

There is a large measure of truth in this geo-strategic explanation. Contemporaries understood its force and it only became overlaid as a result of the religious passions that ruled Holland in the centuries after the Revolt. Calvinist school text books had created an ortho-doxy that the Revolt was a manifest *Dutch* destiny. Yet, like the 'protestant' interpretation, the new one also drew its strength from the passions of visionaries – in this case the prophets of a 'great Netherlands' movement – who insisted above all on emphasising the original unity of the *whole* Netherlands to which they wished to return. Accordingly they tended to diminish the importance of any inherent separative factors dividing Netherlandish north from Netherlandish south. This desire to obliterate evidence of any fundamental differences between north and south *before* the Revolt led them to ignore, or underestimate, other factors and contingencies of great importance, political, social and personal.

It is not, for example, by any means certain that the 'river-line' defence would have saved Holland if both Alba and later his successor Parma had not been called away at a crucial juncture to deal with events in France. The defeat of the Spanish Armada in 1588 was another turning point in the war. Secondly, the collapse of the united Netherlands resistance to Spain in 1579 does seem after all to have been connected with the continued predominance in the south of a feudal nobility, quarrelsome, jealous, unamenable to discipline. In social structure, north and south differed markedly. While the middle class rose in the north, it sank in the south. Finally, there is the providential emergence of one of the most remarkable political figures of the age: William of Orange.

William the Silent, as he came later to be called, was, like most of the Netherlands nobility, not Dutch. Of German blood (as the Dutch national anthem still proclaims) he owned great estates in the Netherlands, France and Germany. It was only with reluctance that he came to lead a revolt against his suzerain, but once committed he threw into the battle all his vigour, political genius, and human understanding, to say nothing of his private fortune. In courage, intelligence and integrity he towered head and shoulders above the other contenders for power. Against all expectation, he managed to hold together the inherently conflicting energies of nobility, regents and Calvinists long enough to give the north its chance to survive. Calvinist support he secured in large measure by adopting the Calvinist religion (1573). From amongst the regents he drew some of his closest advisers. He numbered many of the nobility amongst his friends. Yet as time went on, it became clear that his strongest and most dependable support was geographically in Holland and Zeeland, widely spread amongst the middle classes and common people.

Even before his assassination in 1584 at Delft by Balthasar Gerards, it began to be clear that the nobles of the south were gravitating back towards Spain. It was scarcely any easier to preserve the precarious alliance of the merchant rulers of the cities and the Calvinists, even in the north. For the merchants, latitudinarian, empirically tolerant, had not fought off the threat of the Inquisition only to find themselves shackled by a persecuting theocracy of

Calvinists. Between Catholics and Calvinists they represented a 'Third Force' whose liberalism was to influence the new state decisively. The open split between these two supports of rebellion was nevertheless postponed, not least by William's political sagacity, until after the truce with Spain in 1609: until in fact the Republic was established. The long devotion of the Dutch people to the House of Orange was well founded.

Thus geography, strategy, the brilliant exploits of the Sea-Beggars, the political genius of William, the systematic generalship of his son, Maurice, the good fortune of contingencies such as the Armada – all help to explain the emergence of the Republic. Yet if we ask ourselves what *caused* the people of the northern provinces to offer this protracted resistance to their overlord, to think it worth while to pour out blood and treasure, and so, in the end, survive to found a unique society quite different in government, economy, outlook and ideology from anything else in the modern world, we are still left with a feeling of inadequacy. What *were* they fighting for? Perhaps one key to the stubborn *power* behind Dutch resistance may be found in the personality of one of the greatest intellectual figures of the century: Erasmus of Rotterdam.

Erasmus is invariably thought of as an international, European, cosmopolitan figure, a wandering scholar in the medieval tradition, product of Paris, Louvain, Basle, Freibourg, Oxford, Cambridge. His languages were Greek and Latin and in these his reputation was made. His native country and fellow countrymen he deserted, describing them more than once in terms exceedingly unflattering. Like many Dutchmen since, Erasmus wanted to burst out of his small corner of Holland. The world was his study. He wanted to breathe the air of Europe, not merely of Holland. All this is true, and yet he remained in many essentials characteristically Dutch. The wit and satire of his *Praise of Folly* is recognisably Dutch, at once blunt and delicate. Few writers have ever etched their own personality, including their human weaknesses, into their letters as Erasmus did; his literary technique of portraiture reminds us irresistibly of the observational technique of the Netherlands' painters. When he looks into his own soul it is as if we are looking through the eye that created the Rembrandt self-portraits:

In my youth long ago I would shiver at the very name of death. This at least I have achieved as I have grown older, that I do not greatly fear death, and I do not measure man's happiness by number of days . . . perhaps if as the poets tell jealousy falls silent after death, fame will shine out the more brightly: although it ill becomes a Christian heart to be moved by human glory; may I have the glory of pleasing Christ![1]

A pen picture of Thomas More which he sends to his then friend Ulrich von Hutten could as easily have come from the brush of Breughel:

His right shoulder seems a little higher than the left, particularly when he is walking: this is not natural to him but due to force of habit, like many of the little habits which we pick up. There is nothing to strike one in the rest of his body; only his hands are somewhat clumsy . . .[2]

In his faith in moral education and tolerance, in peace, humanity and kindliness, Erasmus looked ahead to the 'perfectibility' thinkers – to Rousseau and nineteenth century liberalism. No adjective has been more used than 'Erasmian' to describe the relative latitudinarianism to which men in the Netherlands looked back a few years later when Lutherans, Calvinists, Catholics, inspired by reform and counter-reform, tortured, burnt and massacred each other without mercy in the name of Christ. There have always been those who find Erasmus's willingness to compromise and his innate conservatism unimpressive compared with the furious positive activity of the reforms from whom he broke away. Yet his own words are a not unworthy justification:

I bear with this Church until I shall see a better and it cannot help bearing with me until I shall myself be better. And he does not sail badly who steers a middle course between two several evils.[3]

As a scholar and humanist dedicated to preserving peace, to rediscovering antiquity and through antiquity truth, to lambasting the corruption of bishops and the ignorance of the clergy, Erasmus stood on the side-lines of history. His influence in the Netherlands and throughout Europe was nevertheless enormous even in his own lifetime. One Dutch historian even tried to attribute the Dutch Revolt itself to his attacks on bad princes. That is to exaggerate. But there was much of the Erasmian spirit in the work and life of the great leader of the Dutch revolt, William the Silent. It must often have seemed, in the stormiest periods, as William spoke quietly, rationally, and without bitterness or chagrin to his colleagues, to visiting diplomats, to common soldiers in Antwerp or the children in the streets of Delft, that these were echoes of the authentic voice and mind of Erasmus.

Much of this Erasmianism flowed down to the class of regent-magistrates who steadily came to rule the cities of the new Republic and therefore the Republic itself. In Oldenbarneveldt, the first great civil leader of the Republic, in Grotius, its voice and brain on many great political, diplomatic and legal occasions, in Johan de Witt, its leader for twenty crucial years from 1653, one can sense the Erasmian strain, the belief in reason and rational argument as a means of moral improvement and a way of life. While Calvinist pastors were still demanding that witches be burnt alive, the new ruling class of Holland put a stop to the practice, a century earlier than elsewhere.

The great Dutch historian Huizinga, used to claim that the history of Holland had been less bloody and cruel than that of surrounding countries.

Not for naught did Erasmus praise as truly Dutch those qualities which we might also call truly Erasmian: gentleness, kindliness, moderation, a generally diffused moderate erudition. Not romantic virtues, if you like; but are they the less salutary?[4]

Later generations can ponder their answer. Erasmus was in part the product of the old Burgundian tradition. Through his struggle against religious obscurantism, through his humanism, through his own vivid, fastidious personality, he helped to prolong and preserve his own ideals through a period when they came under ferocious attack from bigots on both sides of the religious fence. They were ideals well suited to the new bourgeois state of the Republic which they helped to inspire. The Republic in its turn – or at any rate its powerful ruling magistrate class – was well equipped to preserve, cherish and transmit these Erasmian ideals. Calvinism was on the attack in the new state from its beginning onwards for a century and three quarters. But it was held in check by the cautious Erasmian obstinacy of the ruling merchant class. Freedom of thought, in a remarkable degree, was preserved. Europe in the seventeenth and eighteenth centuries was to owe an incalculable debt to the Erasmian tradition and to the dominant class in the Dutch Republic by whose efforts it was protected. In the mind and spirit of Erasmus lies the key to the understanding of much later Dutch history. Counter-reformation fanaticism was check-mated by Calvinist fanaticism in the struggle for Dutch independence. But Erasmianism played a no less vital role in this, the first decisive defeat of dynasticism rampant and the establishment of a middle-class Republic.

Finally, we shall fail to understand much of the subsequent history of the Dutch Republic if we fail to observe that from the beginning it was a pivot of internationalism – in its alliances and conflicts, its economy and culture. It was born out of international wars at the cross-roads of Europe in which Spain and France were chiefly involved. The civil wars in France were especially important for the outcome of the Dutch rebellion, for Huguenot successes in France threatened occupying Spanish troops in the Netherlands. Ultimately, though with extreme reluctance, Elizabeth of England was drawn into the struggle. After a long period during which Spain, France and England manoeuvred for position in the Netherlands, the last decade of the century steadily brought together the Dutch rebels in alliance with both France and England. It was the success of Henri IV against his enemies in France which, as much as anything, enabled the Dutch to conclude the truce with Spain in 1609. The truce itself was negotiated by the skilful Jeannin, Henri IV's Ambassador to the Low Countries, who had already steered through the peace treaty between France and Spain.

After that it was no longer possible for France to furnish official military aid to the rebels. But scores of young French nobles continued to fight in the Netherlands. The sons of Sully, of Duplessis-Mornay, the 'Protestant Pope', the Count of Chatillon, and many others, died in battle there, as Sir Philip Sidney had died earlier at the siege of Zutfen. Down to the accession of Louis XIV, the Republic owed much to the French alliance. But the treaty of the Pyrenees (1659) which annexed Artois to France and gave her strong points in Hainault, Flanders and Luxembourg threw a shadow over the century-old alliance. It was soon to darken into war.

The international conflict in which the new Republic was cradled was not merely one of diplomatists and soldiers. These were, as Sir George Clark has said, 'episodes in a single war of ideas.' The political controversies were international. The most celebrated justification of rebellion of the age, the *Vindiciae contra Tyrannos* of 1579, shows how international was the traffic in political ideas. It deals mainly with events in France, and is sometimes regarded as a French work. But the two most likely authors, Languet and

Duplessis-Mornay, were close friends of William of Orange and the work itself portrays France and the Netherlands as adjacent theatres of war and ideological conflict. William's personal ties with France were strong: quite apart from his own stake in Orange, he took as his third wife a Bourbon-Montpensier, and a Coligny, daughter of the great Huguenot Admiral, as his fourth.

Calvinism was yet another internationalising influence. Netherlands Calvinism came from France, through the Walloon Provinces that stood between the Netherlands and France. Although these provinces later became 'obedient' to Spain or part of France, they provided in the 1560s and 1570s some of the most zealous supporters of Protestantism. Walloon Protestant churches continued to exist throughout the Republic (some still do) conducting Calvinist services in French. Even in England and Scotland, the 'Dutch' immigrant colonies often worshipped in the French tongue. And after the Edict of Nantes was revoked in 1685 and the French colonies in England and Holland were once again enlarged, ties were immediately re-formed between the French and Dutch again. It is impossible after 1700 to disentangle Huguenot and Dutch family relationships in the City of London.

The world of letters was another facet of this international community. The new intelligentsia that helped to rule the rebellious cities of Holland from 1572 onwards had wide international sympathies. Humanists, poets, administrators and patriots like Jan van Hout and Jan Dousa of Leyden looked both to France and England. The new University founded to celebrate the breaking of the Spaniards' siege of Leyden in 1574 had its roots in French culture. Its early scholars had studied in Paris, admired the works of Ronsard, Du Bartas, Du Bellay. Wealthy Dutch merchants continued to send their sons to France to educate themselves and perfect their knowledge of a language which was indispensable to them whether they became diplomats, merchants or scholars.

Oldenbarneveldt studied at Bourges, many others at Paris. It was therefore natural that William of Orange should appoint distinguished French scholars to the first chairs at Leyden – Louis Cappel of Paris, Guillaume Feugueray of Rouen. Among the French *maîtres* recruited to Leyden in the late sixteenth century none was greater than the great classical scholar and critic, Scaliger. Born at Agen, he had studied at Bordeaux, Paris and Geneva. Italy and England he visited, disliked and left. Scotland he tolerated, but at Leyden he settled, quarrelling however as violently here as elsewhere. But it was wandering, independent spirits like Scaliger that gave Leyden its reputation. By his time its international student body included thirty-seven French students. Amongst them were names that were to be famous later – the biblical scholar Guez de Balzac and the poet Théophile de Viau.

The rebel provinces comprised, then, a *pays sans frontières*. The seeds of tolerance and freedom that had been latent through the Burgundian era of noble, ecclesiastical and municipal privileges and 'liberties' now burgeoned with fresh vigour. They were nourished by the new freedoms accorded to industry and trade, to immigrant capital, labour and money, to religion and ideas. The constitution of the new State seemed to many supposedly wise and experienced contemporaries elsewhere to be an impossibility. How could a motley collection of tradesmen, salt dealers, fishermen and tallow chandlers hope to govern themselves without royal or even noble guidance? The Dutch were in no way perturbed. A few years before she died, Queen Elizabeth, for long chief of the sceptics, admitted her conversion. This sagacious administration, she told the Dutch ambassador, was

so full of good order and policy so to surpass by far in its wisdom the intelligence of all kings and potentates. We kings require – all of us – to go to school to the States General.[5]

2 Economic growth and economic rivalry

After forty years of war the underlying economic strength of the northern Netherlands had never been greater than it was at the truce of 1609. So far from being weakened by the drain of money, the merchants of the new state had seen their business grow and expand. In the mid sixteenth century, Amsterdam was only one trading town among many others. Like the other cities of the north it was inferior to Antwerp, even to Ghent. To Thomas Gresham, Queen Elizabeth's agent, it was noteworthy only as a place where you went to buy wainscoting. As late as 1577 it was still dominated by a Roman Catholic élite that kept it loyal to Spain in defiance of the rebels of Leyden and the other great cities of Holland, Zeeland and Flanders. The *coup d'état* of 1578 changed all this. In the twenty years after it joined the revolt in that year, the economic power of Amsterdam waxed exceedingly. By the time of the truce it had already begun to assume some of the features that were to make it by the mid century the centre of a network of world trade and finance. A century later Daniel Defoe wrote a classic description of the economic functions of the Dutch Republic in the contemporary world.

The Dutch must be understood as they really are, the Middle Persons in Trade, the Factors and Brokers of Europe . . . they *buy* to *sell* again, *take* in to *send* out, and the greatest Part of their vast Commerce consists in being supply'd from All Parts of the World, that they may supply All the World again.[6]

This was as good an analysis of the Dutch entrepôt as one could have. The late sixteenth century had witnessed two new phenomena, one demographic, one technological. Throughout Europe there was one of those population explosions which from time to time characterise human society. Its origins are still obscure; its consequences clear. In many countries, even in those areas of the Mediterranean that had once produced food surpluses for neighbours, poverty and starvation now threatened millions of people.

The *Fluit* (flute or flyboat, as it was known) was the
greatest innovation of marine technology of the sixteenth and
seventeenth centuries. Built specifically as a cheap freighter,
it gave the Dutch mastery of the bulk cargo trades at sea
from its first appearance at the Hoorn shipyards in the 1590s.
Painting by A. van Salm, National Maritime Museum, Greenwich.

Yet disaster for the inert and passive was opportunity for the
enterprising, and the Dutch swiftly seized their chance. They were
already experienced shippers and traders in the seas between the
Baltic and the Bay of Biscay. Already they handled vast cargoes of
grain from the prairies of north Germany and the Eastland, iron
and copper from Sweden, timber from Norway. These they traded
against precious cargoes of salt from Biscay and Portugal and
herrings from the North Sea. This was the backbone of the Dutch
system of trade – the 'spine', the 'mother trade', the 'vital nerve' as it
was variously described.

As the rebels entrenched themselves more firmly in their redoubt north of the great estuaries of Rhine, Scheldt and Maas, this trading system entered a phase of explosive expansion. Now a new technological weapon was deployed. This was a novel type of merchant ship, the *fluit* (flute or flyboat to the English). The flyboat was a seagoing barge, round in the stern, broad bottomed, narrow in deck, cheap to build and operate. Its design was specially suited to the northern trades, but it was not long before it was operating in the Mediterranean, carrying Baltic grain to the hungry peoples of Sicily and the Levant. By the seventeenth century it had become the symbol of Dutch maritime supremacy not only in Europe but in the East Indies too, where it supplemented in local trades the basic functions of the great ships that plied from Amsterdam and Middelburg to India, Ceylon, Java and as far as China and Japan.

The years after the truce (1609) saw the entire Dutch economy surging forward again. The foundations of a great Eastern empire of trade were laid and the colonial monopoly of Spain and Portugal challenged in India and Central America. Calvinist zealots, many of them former rebels from the Southern Provinces, created a West

The principal function of the Amsterdam Exchange Bank
(1609) was to enable merchants to settle mutual debts.
It did not normally lend money. This was the business
of the Loan (Lombard, Leening) Bank (1614). Most of
its capital was deposited by private investors and lent
out to traders in the form of credits or loans.

Indies Company specifically to outface popery in America and
people its east coast with sound Dutch Protestants. Economic
success it never was, but it left an enduring mark in the shape of the
colony of New Amsterdam, later captured and renamed New York
by the English.

While exploration, discovery and trade were rapidly expanding
the area and volume of Dutch overseas trade, the central mechanism of the new economy was being transformed. Immediately
after the truce, an Exchange Bank was created at Amsterdam to
meet the needs of Dutch traders for a convenient means of settling
their accounts. The Bank, like many Dutch institutions, was not as
original an innovation as has sometimes been supposed. Like
marine insurance, double-entry book keeping and many other
techniques of business it was copied from an Italian model – in this
case the Bank of Venice. It was not a note-issuing bank as the
Bank of England was to be: the merchant client paid into his
account and took out what he needed. He did not borrow. Strictly,
the Bank was supposed to make no loans (although in practice it
was to do so as time passed). This was the function of another
institution, the Loan Bank, likewise based on an Italian model. But
the essential symbol of the expanding economy was the Bourse.

The elegant classical building and courtyard designed by Hendrik de Keyser in 1609 was the mirror and microcosm of the world
trading network of the Republic. Each one of the thirty or more
stone pillars that supported its cloistered sidewalks became the
chartered meeting place for a specific group of merchants: here the
East India merchants would foregather, there the Levant or Baltic
dealers. At another you could charter a ship or insure its cargo.
And outside in the open court the talk was of stocks and shares,
speculations and deals in 'futures'. This was the special business of
a growing community of Spanish and Portuguese Jews. For half a
century or more these refugees from Spanish persecution had been

trickling into the Republic, to Amsterdam especially, from their first haven of refuge in Antwerp. Not as yet a rich or powerful community, but already solid enough to build a splendid synagogue that remains one of the great architectural glories of the city; soon to produce one of the most disturbing intellectual influences of the century, Spinoza, and provide in its quarter of the city a home and friends for Rembrandt.

The polyglot character of the growing city reflected in part the political upheavals of the previous half century that had attracted refugees from many quarters of Europe to its relatively liberal franchise. Yet its liberalism and tolerance were empirical, reflecting in turn a fairly practical concern for its success as an *emporium*. Like all the great *emporia* of the past – Athens, Marseilles, Venice, Antwerp – Amsterdam was full of strangers. By 1622 it was reckoned that a third of its total population – now over 100,000 – consisted of immigrants from the southern Netherlands and their first generation descendants. Their beliefs and customs were as varied as their merchandise and currencies.

The Jewish quarter of Amsterdam in the seventeenth century, home of the Sephardic (Portuguese) Jews who had fled from the Inquisition. It was not originally a rich community, but gradually its members penetrated many trades and professions, enjoyed a rich cultural life with men among them such as Rembrandt and Spinoza, and built the superb synagogue of 1600. The synagogue in Amsterdam was copied a century later at Bevis Marks, London, by Sephardic immigrants.

> Hence Amsterdam – Turk, Christian, Pagan, Jew,
> Staple of sects and mint of schism grew:
> That bank of conscience where not one so strange
> Opinion but finds credit and exchange.[7]

Marvell's elaborate and extended versified play on the Dutch was not intended as a compliment. But it illustrates the impact made by this novel, unique society that put itself at the disposal of trade and was itself the creation of trade, evolving freely and spontaneously in response to economic opportunities and pressures. Steadily it freed itself from feudal and dynastic influences and skilfully avoided the traps set by new forms of Calvinist religious fanaticism. Impediments to the free flow of trade were fewer here than anywhere in the contemporary world; the Amsterdam citizen might have justly claimed, as Pericles had claimed for Athens: 'Because of the greatness of our city the fruits of the whole earth flow in upon us'.

As the seventeenth century went on, its quays and wharves were equipped generously with moving cranes and lighters. Its warehouses were stocked with Baltic grain, rolls of English woollen textiles, silks and spices from India, sugar from Brazil and the West Indies, iron and timber from Scandinavia, wine from Germany, barrels of salted herrings caught off the coasts of England and Scotland, coal from Newcastle, malting barley from Norfolk. Hardly a country that was not drawn ineluctably into the tightening network of Dutch trade and credit by the skill, experience and technology that for a time placed this economy apart from the agrarian backwardness of the rest.

The supreme irony was provided by Spain. Ossified, decayed, overloaded with a grievous burden of war taxes and loans, chronically suffering an insoluble balance of payments problem, the would-be Spanish conquerors were forced to pay tribute to the Dutch through trading with this enemy who alone could supply them and

The of
Towne of Ams

their colonies with the basic foods and manufactured goods necessary to their very existence. Thus Amsterdam became not only the centre of a system that financed trade in the settled areas of Europe through credit instruments: it also pre-empted a sizeable proportion of the silver that Spain drew from Central America, long before it reached the mother country. Succeeding years in the seventeenth century saw the Spanish Silver Fleet moving under heavy convoy from Spain, up the English Channel to the Zuider Zee, eloquent tribute to the economic grip which the Dutch rebels had obtained on Spain and her empire.

It is sometimes suggested that this was a purely commercial economy that somehow failed to change gear into a phase of industrialisation. In so far as it missed any true Industrial Revolution until very late, there is a measure of truth in this view. Yet as far as seventeenth century conditions are concerned it is an exaggeration. Nothing was more characteristic of the new Republic than a large group of medium-sized cities and ports – Leyden, Haarlem, Gouda, Middelburg, Enkhuizen. There were more of such towns, with populations ranging from 20,000 to 40,000, than in England, France or Germany. They were in part commercial, but their citizenry, often immigrant, commanded the accumulated industrial skills drawn from all the corners of the Netherlands as a whole; and they gave a special flavour to the Republic. Much of the technology represented here was rationally concentrated on those economically highly profitable processes for finishing or refining raw materials or semi-manufactured products; this stimulated the flow of goods through the warehouses and markets. Haarlem became the centre where coarse linens from Germany were bleached and finished. With men and skills borrowed from Antwerp, Amsterdam dyed and dressed semi-finished cloths imported 'in the white' from England. Leyden, its ancient textile industries in decay by 1572, was revitalised after the siege by Southern Netherlands' immigrants to become the largest manufacturing centre of the so-called 'New Draperies' of seventeenth-century Europe.

Such developments represented a calculated attack on potential markets for new products. A growing urban population throughout Europe might need a brighter, lighter, more sophisticated, cheaper type of cloth for wear or furnishing; Leyden would produce it. War might destroy old markets in northern Europe: the Dutch would seek out new markets in the Mediterranean and beat the Venetians at their own game. Where did the biggest profit margins lie in textile manufacture? Not in spinning or weaving or growing wool but in the refined technology of dyeing and dressing the cloth which provided the key to the control of the markets. Hence a grip on the English cloth industry, much resented in England. From 1614 to 1622 a group of London merchants led by a former lord mayor, Alderman Cokayne, tried to break the Dutch grip by forbidding the export of undyed cloth and promoting the dyeing industry in London. They failed, with disastrous results that shook English industry for forty years.

Other industries at Amsterdam, Delft and elsewhere worked on similar principles – sugar refining, malting, distilling, brewing, tobacco cutting, silk throwing, pottery, glass, armament manufacture, printing, paper making. Many of these skills came originally from the South Netherlands. They were now developed in the North. Apart from ship-building, there was little that could be called heavy industry. Except in certain branches of the Leyden cloth industry, machinery was uncommon and was largely limited to hand-operated looms. Yet these were the forms of industry most appropriate to a land whose natural resources were virtually nil. It was characteristic of the Dutch capacity for realistic response to the facts of economic life that they concentrated on industries that utilised imported materials or semi-finished goods, yielded very high rates of profit and provided effective control of the market at the expense (as it often seemed) of less developed nations.

The economy thus contrived reached its peak about the middle years of the seventeenth century: or should we say its 'plateau'? For there was no sudden decline. Political crises might cause economic anxieties, as they did in the 1650s or 1670s, when first England and then France took up the role (earlier played by Spain) of aggressor against this all-too-efficient economic rival. But these depressions were temporary. Trade relatively quickly resumed its former level. Former level: a time was to come, after 1730, when it was to become clear that while there was no *absolute* decline, other nations – England and France especially – were growing at a rate that would soon dwarf the Dutch scale of operations. The reasons for this are discussed in a later chapter. For the moment, and for nearly another century, observers in other parts of Europe, from England eastwards to Prussia and Russia, from Sweden south to Spain, were to pay genuine if reluctant tribute to this economic paragon among the nations.

Dutch expertise was alternately regarded in the outside world as a profound mystery beyond the comprehension of less gifted operators, or as a shameless and unjustifiable exploitation of the needs of others which could be easily rectified with a little courage, foresight and policy. Nobody loves a middleman. To their enemies the Dutch had magnified on a national scale those iniquities of self-interest, greed and usury which the Church had condemned through the Middle Ages. Thus resentment, irritation and admiration vied with each other; speculation and hypothesis solidified into anti-Dutch propaganda, anti-Dutch policies and anti-Dutch wars, as the putative victims of Dutch ingenuity, enterprise and diligence sought to throw off the para-colonial Dutch yoke.

In England the seeds of hostility were sown in the classic formulation of a national economic policy by a London merchant, Thomas Mun. Hatched in the discussions round the economic crisis that culminated in England about 1622, Mun's *England's Treasure by Foreign Trade* came in handy forty years later as a ranging shot in the cold war of 1664 as tempers were rising, or being deliberately raised, against the Dutch rival. Its basic theme was the need to compete with the Dutch: by fair means if possible, otherwise by foul, and by force. The Dutch were represented as the obstacle to England's economic progress. The English must make, grow, fish, diversify. At all costs the national product must expand, exports grow, imports diminish. (The theme is still monotonously with us; every decade of the twentieth century hears the same mercantilist story repeated with varying degrees of supposed originality.)

In 1665 (the year after Mun's book was posthumously published), Josiah Child, a prominent London merchant temporarily isolated by the plague, wrote his *Brief Observations Concerning Trade and the Interest of Money*. His theme was 'the prodigious increase of the Netherlands'. Their

> riches and multitude of shipping is the envy of the present and may be the wonder of all future generations: and yet the means whereby they have advanced themselves are sufficiently obvious and in a great measure imitable by most other nations, but more easily by us of this Kingdom of England.

What was the recipe? A list of fifteen ingredients – educational, sociological, technological. The Dutch traded honestly and methodically. They taught accounting and book-keeping in school; they encouraged invention, banks, rationally legal methods of settling disputes and debts. Above all, they saw to it that practical businessmen played a suitably prominent part in the councils of the nation where policy was shaped. All this had achieved economic results that could be summarised in one phenomenon: a rate of interest of three per cent – half that which prevailed in England.

> This [said Child] in my poor opinion is the *causa causans* of all the other

causes of riches in that people; and if interest of money were with us reduced to the same rate as it is with them, it would in a short time render us rich and considerable in trade as they now are.

The grand solution was perhaps a little oversimplified. But plenty of distinguished economists were to fall into the same trap in later history.

A broader survey of Dutch economy and society at first hand was the influential *Observations on the United Provinces* by Sir William Temple (1673). Temple, like another earlier – though less friendly – observer, Sir George Downing, served as ambassador in Holland. His work was to remain a standard authority on the subject. Like Child, he was struck by the low rate of interest in Holland that caused 'so much money to lye ready for all Projects by which gain may be expected'. He too listed the practical conveniences that Dutchmen contrived for trade – banks, laws, freedom from interference, and so on. Their success was not accidental or evanescent. It resulted from 'a great concurrence of circumstances, a long course of Time, force of Orders and Method, which never before met in the World to such a degree, or with so prodigious a success and perhaps never will again!'

On one point, Temple was to be vigorously challenged by a later writer. Bernard Mandeville, the author of *The Fable of the Bees, or Private Vices, Public Benefits*, was a medical practitioner, Dutch by birth and training, who settled in London but was compelled (if rumour was correct) to eke out his professional income by writing for the distillers 'in defence of spirituous liquors'. His major work was a set of provocative arabesques on the theme that *luxury* is the best foundation for a flourishing and healthy society. He accordingly quarrelled with Temple's view that the foundation of Dutch prosperity (now threatened by excessive luxury) was 'thrift and parsimony' crystallised in savings. *Luxury* (said Mandeville) was its basis. Temple's gloomy prophecies were unfulfilled after nearly half a century. Holland remained a land of luxury and prosperity.

Mandeville's later disciples included Dr Johnson, who was encouraged by his reading of Mandeville always stoutly to defend luxury as a source of prosperity and social welfare. Maynard Keynes likewise owed not a little to Mandeville's belief in luxury as an economic stimulant. The truth was dismally ambiguous. Some Dutch saved; others spent and consumed conspicuously. But sheer lack of space prevented them from setting up as a *nouveau riche* rural aristocracy. Their merchants and bankers did not take to the hunt, or lock up their money in vast estates or family ambitions. They remained, by and large, an urban oligarchy closely attached to trade if not actively in it.

The English were not the only observers to envy and admire the Dutch and probe their secrets. One of the best descriptions of the Dutch trade of the late seventeenth century came from France, from the pen of Daniel Huet, Bishop of Avranches. It was not so odd as it might seem that a French bishop should turn economist. Huet's *Le Grand Trésor Historique et Politique du Florissent Commerce des Hollandois dans Tous les Etats et Empires du Monde* first appeared in 1694, at the end of the great famine in France. It was republished several times and translated into English and other languages. Huet was a friend of Fénélon, Archbishop of Cambrai, and a member of a group of influential people centring round Fénélon who were strongly opposed to much French government policy. They believed in particular that the nationalist economic policies based on rigid government direction of economic affairs, inaugurated by Colbert and continued under his son Seignelay and others, had been disastrous for France. They had wrecked the chances of a fruitful trade treaty with the Dutch. They had led to trade quarrels which had partly caused the disastrous Franco-Dutch wars. These had stopped trade for seven years, taught the

Dutch how to do without French products and increased, not lessened, their strength.

But besides the immediate implications of State *dirigisme* there were deeper ones. For Huet the *dirigisme* of Louis and Colbert was not only foolish and impracticable: it was morally and theologically unsound. Huet was also the voice of protest speaking for a group of ecclesiastical and secular magnates who saw current policies of centralised government control in France as an attack on the sacred rights of Church and nobility as well as of merchants. Hence the significance of the Dutch Republic, which had arisen out of resistance to a similar attempt by the King of Spain to impose his will against all historic precedent. Far from being intimidated or depressed, the new Dutch nation had emerged stronger and more prosperous than ever. For this French opposition, therefore, the Dutch, representing free enterprise and individual rights as opposed to the immoral *étatisme* of France, were a proper subject of enquiry and admiration.

Even in Spain the second quarter of the eighteenth century heard voices raised against the torpor and stupidity of national economic policy. Geronymo de Uztariz (1689–1757) and Bernardo Ulloa, a contemporary, were the prophets of a new, rational mercantilism, which would set up commercial skill and technology against the crazy, inverted fiscalism that taxed exports, hampered manufacturers and generally killed what it was supposed to nurture. But their model and cynosure was still the Dutch. Perhaps by this time it was a little out of date. But Spaniards at any rate still supposed they could learn from it. So too in their different ways did the Enlightened Despots. More practical than the scribblers and philosophers, Peter the Great visited the shipyards of Zaandam for himself to see how it was all done. Half a century later Frederick the Great was still quoting the Dutch as examples of successful economic method; ironically, he was at the same time inaugurating

The 'East Indiamen' were the largest and finest
of the great Dutch merchant fleet, heavily armed
and manned. A fine drawing by the Czech
draughtsman Wenceslas Hollar, who settled
in England but fled as a royalist to the Low Countries
in the English civil war (1641–60).

tollandica, per Indias Orientales

Prussian policies of economic development which were the antithesis of Dutch ideas.

From the mid seventeenth century the Dutch economic miracle came in for scrutiny, sometimes admiring, often hostile, as one state after another passed over to policies of economic nationalism designed to eliminate Dutch middlemen from their economies. The pioneers were the English. From 1651, by a combination of Navigation Laws, naval wars, protective tariffs, subsidies, bounties, and privileged immigration, they went over to the attack. The theme of English 'mercantilism' was consistent: increase exports, diminish imports, reserve local materials for local producers, buy skilled labour, stop Dutch middlemen and ship-operators from intruding into fields that the English could exploit for themselves. Hence a series of blows – undoubtedly effective though never fatal – against Dutch trade and shipping. After the Restoration in 1660 restrictions were tightened still further. Meanwhile, Colbert, fanatically determined to extrude the Dutch from the French economy, had set up tariffs against Dutch imports, and in 1672 loyally supported his royal master's plans for an all-out attack on the Dutch Republic and its trade.

As one nation after another devised its measures against the Dutch, it became clear how perilously exposed they were to reprisals. Economic innovations are invariably short lived, fatally easy to imitate. As the world demographic pressure on food supplies lessened, as better methods of transport – shipping especially – became more familiar, new agricultural techniques more widespread, the Dutch economic lead shortened. As early as the first English war (1652–4) the Dutch admirals were complaining that their task was impossible. To win, they had to smash the English fleet before it smashed them and destroyed the far-flung Dutch merchant navy and fishing fleet. Yet how could they be expected to do this and simultaneously convoy straggling flocks of unarmed flyboats through the Channel and the narrow seas of Europe?

It became clear that there was no easy solution to the Dutch problems of economy and defence in a world where practically every year was a year of war. 'Profit and Power,' Josiah Child observed, 'must jointly be considered.' Ever since the revolt against Alba and the Tenth Penny in 1569, the Dutch merchants had set themselves up to pursue economically rational policies. Not for them the idiocies of dynasticism, war, persecution. They had managed to learn their own lessons admirably. But how to persuade others? The Spaniards they had worn down, with the help (among others) of Queen Elizabeth, Henri IV, Richelieu and Providence. The English and the French were a much tougher proposition. Diplomatic ingenuity, neutrality or non-involvement could (and did) achieve much. They could not achieve all. Some basic, and ugly, facts remained to be faced.

Amongst the very much larger nations of Europe – the twenty million French and six million English – the one to two million Dutch were trying to operate a unique kind of economy. Uniquely profitable, rational and commercially efficient it was also uniquely vulnerable, exposed and extended. Long lines of communication at sea had to be defended against attack; unarmed ships of trade shepherded through narrow seas against attacks by enemy forces, pirates, privateers. The boundaries of the Republic resulting from war could only be defended by disastrously expensive flooding operations. Manpower was scarce; mercenaries expensive and unsatisfactory. The Eighty Years War (1567–1648) had delivered the Dutch heroically but expensively from the threat of Spanish dynasticism: the European Wars (from 1664–1714) from French hegemony. Yet by the eighteenth century men were beginning to ask whether the resulting burden was really supportable. The 'Periwig Period' in Holland was one of social and economic *malaise*. To many, Dutch society seemed a clumsy bourgeois *pastiche* of French culture. It was even rumoured (no doubt with encouragement from Huguenot refugees) that Madame de Maintenon had advised Louis xiv to spread French luxuries in the United Provinces so as to ruin its economy. Moralists like Van der Goes denounced these gallicisms. Were his compatriots mere chameleons? But Dutch society continued to be immensely receptive and absorptive. Terms like *pourpoint, baudrier, chemise*, and many others relating to couture passed into Dutch. The Netherlands had, after all, been impregnated with French ideas, customs and habits since the Middle Ages. *Pays sans frontières*, it was inevitable that Holland should respond freely to the new age of French influence.

3 A middle-class society

The successful revolt against Spain not only released the great economic energies of the new Republic: it also revolutionised the nature of Dutch society and altered radically the balance of political forces in the Republic. As power in the city governments passed from the old Catholic oligarchy to the Protestant *élite*, a new ruling merchant class steadily moved to the front of the political stage. The political eclipse of the old aristocracy was more gradual and less pronounced in the landward provinces than in Holland and Zeeland. In Gelderland and Overijssel old families continued to live in their medieval castles and enjoy their medieval privileges. In Holland, the rural 'gentry' were new arrivals, their most plausible claims to titles either foreign or derived from the recent purchase out of trading profits of a few ancient manorial rights. Their real home was the town. Trade was the source of their wealth and influence. It was this 'social dictatorship of the merchant class', as it has been described, that made the new Republic, its economy and its policies, unique in a world still largely governed elsewhere by princes and guided by the dynastic values of a feudal class.

Descartes, like many other refugees from the troubles elsewhere, spent much of his life (1596–1650) in Holland. He remarked more than once on the dominance there of trade, the profit motive and private advantage among its citizens. How unlike the old societies where social prestige derived still from tradition, family and land:

In this great town [he wrote from Amsterdam] where apart from myself there dwells no one who is not engaged in trade, everyone is so much out for his own advantage that I should be able to live my whole life here without ever meeting a mortal being.[8]

Outsiders thought the same. To Charles I the government of his new Republic seemed 'a populace, without discretion' – a *hoi polloi* of brewers, bakers and felt-makers. Yet in fact the descendants of the working tanners and soap-boilers of only a generation or two back were by now a mercantile *élite*. As Amsterdam grew in its unique pattern of canals built in concentric half-circles, the great merchant-regent families – the Bickers, Pels, De Graeffs, Trips, De Geers and scores of others – built houses of princely size and pomp along the Heerengracht and Singel. Outside the city, a few bought country seats, finely designed and appointed, on the river Vecht or the reclaimed Beemster.

Many were still actively engaged in trade even in the second half of the seventeenth century, but by then a new trend was marked. Though they mostly remained an urban patriciate, their surplus wealth was going into investment in land. Jacob (Father) Cats, author of those long stretches of homely moralising alexandrines still popular in Zeeland, his native province, was also a regent (magistrate). He ended as pensionary of Dordrecht for thirteen years. In the intervals of reading and writing his verses, Cats, like many of his fellow regents, speculated during the years of the Truce in lands flooded in war and going cheap. He also invested in similar enterprises in England where Dutch engineers were at work in the Fens. But this time he was less successful, saying 'To make dykes is at best an uncertain chance, but this applies particularly to dykes one builds abroad.'

The incident shows nevertheless the regents making use of their political connections and commercial enterprise to combine their interest in trade and land. Andrew Marvell's *Character of Holland* lampooned these engineer rulers of the Republic:

> So rules among the drownèd he that drains:
> Not who first sees the rising sun, commands,
> But who could first drain the rising lands;
> Who best could know to pump an earth so leak,
> Him they their Lord, and Country's Father speak;
> To make a bank, was a great plot of State,
> Invent a shov'l, and be a Magistrate.

Dutch artists sought beauty everywhere, amidst poverty as well as riches. But Samuel van Hoogstraeten (1627–78) was above all the advocate of charm and elegance, here conveyed in this *View Down a Corridor* of a wealthy house such as might be found along the canals of Amsterdam or the Vecht. Towards the end of his life he published a treatise on elegance in art. The National Trust, Dyrham Park, Gloucestershire.

Ordinary business men grumbled continually that the regents had sunk so much money in land and land speculation that they were no longer truly concerned for trade. A *rentier* class was emerging. Aitzema, the historian, writing in 1652, complained that the interests of trade were neglected because 'the *Heeren* (regents) were not merchants, but drew their income from houses, lands and investments.'[9]

Whether (as is often claimed) there was a progressive decline in public morality is less clear. Even early in the century C. P. Hooft, a regent of Amsterdam descended from a long line of skippers and father of a famous poet, complained publicly of the excessive profits made by some of his fellow-governors out of the extensions of the city. His reward for his trouble was to be kept out of office for many years.

More serious for social welfare and the efficiency of government was the trend towards the systematic exploitation of public office which became more pronounced as the century went on. The regents took turns to appoint their friends to jobs. Contracts in writing, known as 'contracts of correspondence' or, more euphemistically, 'contracts of harmony' distributed jobs to the fortunate, while the less fortunate were specifically excluded from any share in the proceedings.

The risks arising from corruption of this kind were obvious. All the more because the rise of the Republic had placed the government of the towns, and such central federal government as there was, firmly in the hands of this upper-middle class of merchants. Apart from a brief flurry of democracy in the 1570s, their power and authority was unchallenged by any other class. Before the Revolt, the central government, Burgundian and Habsburg, had limited the regents' exercise of power to their own towns. A relic of this central authority still survived in the right of the Stadholder to choose certain local magistrates from lists presented to him. But

his latitude was in reality strictly limited. His writ never ran in Amsterdam itself, and in any case fell into abeyance when there was no Stadholder (from 1650–72). Any central check on the local power of the regents thus disappeared.

Theoretically chosen from those citizens who represented all that was best in wisdom, morality and wealth, the regents stayed in office for life unless they went mad or bankrupt. These same families who supplied local officials, burgomasters, pensionaries, secretaries, councillors and aldermen also operated the federal government of the Republic. Under the new constitutional arrangements after the Revolt, the rising power and wealth of the towns of Holland was reflected in the reduced voting strength of the nobility in the provincial and central government. Eighteen towns now had one vote each in the assembly of the provincial states; the nobility, representing the countryside, gave only one collective vote. The provincial states had one vote each in the States General, the most important federal organ of the Republic.

This was not a sovereign body. It acted only on instructions from the provincial states. Some of these, as has been pointed out, still had a strong rural and feudal element, but their influence was far less than that of the dominant, rich and powerful Holland. How should this clumsy, creaking instrument of federalism in which the powers of Stadholder, federal assembly and local governments were so ill-defined and conflicting, ever be able to work?

Like most governments of the age it was inefficient and unsatisfactory. It worked maddeningly slowly, precisely because it represented that ingrained respect for particular and corporate rights that had been a main dynamo of the Revolt against Spain. Such delays could be disastrous where negotiations with foreign powers were concerned. Time and again colonial disputes with England were bedevilled by the failure of the States General to reach agreement on orders to their own officials. Attempts to reach a treaty of alliance with England in 1651 collapsed for the same reason. In wartime, rivalries between local authorities were fatal: the first Anglo-Dutch War showed how impossible it was to divide responsibility for a naval war between five different Admiralties. But in other affairs, especially economic, the creaking federal machine was lubricated by interest, common sense, and the realities of power. Theoretically Overijssel might have the same voting power as Holland in the States General. In practice, the fact that she provided three per cent of the federal revenue, while Holland provided over half, or one fifth more than the other six provinces combined, was reflected in Holland's political predominance in the Republic. This enforced a certain degree of coherence in policy.

The 'social dictatorship' of the upper-middle class in the Republic rested on the social coherence of this class or group of classes. For long they had wielded economic power. As a result of the Revolt they had seized political power. In this respect the Revolt was more like the French Revolution than the English Civil War. The Republic was (to quote Gustav Renier)

a commonwealth of merchants with a medieval constitution but with class relations such as existed elsewhere in Europe in the first half of the nineteenth century, with powerful monarchist instincts that were only half stifled by a republican form of government, with an intense and almost precocious national consciousness, and also with an inherent tendency towards an organisation in which the classes below that which is dominant would be able eventually to achieve their share of power.[10]

The nobility, then, were a dwindling caste, closed and doomed. Now monarchy had gone, there could be no addition to their numbers. Yet there was no unbridgeable social gulf between them and the merchant regents who had replaced them in power in the dominant maritime provinces. Nobles joined the boards of the new commercial companies. They married their daughters to the sons of regents. The regents, though mostly living modestly, even austerely in the first half of the century, were not hostile to the landed gentry. On the contrary, they did their best to acquire a modest degree of status by buying land which gave them the right to use heraldic seals or escutcheons. As time went on, they lived on a grander scale. Their sons went to the universities of Leyden, Utrecht or Groningen, read classics or law and travelled abroad on something like a Grand Tour, returning to follow a predestined career as public administrators.

Politics in the new Republic see-sawed throughout the century between the parties that represented respectively the merchant-regents (the States party or Loevestein faction) and the predomin-antly Calvinist supporters of the House of Orange. The judicial murder of Oldenbarneveldt, first great leader of the States party, in 1619, ended regent predominance; until 1650 the Stadholders Maurice (d. 1625), Frederick Henry (d. 1647), and William II (d. 1650) and their supporters were in power. Then from 1650 to 1672 came a long period when there was no Stadholder. For most of the period Johan de Witt led the regents and the country as grand pensionary. Another period of Orangist rule followed under Willian III, joint ruler of the Republic and of England, until 1701.

What were the issues between the parties that ended in the execution of Oldenbarneveldt and the murder, in most horrible circumstances, of the De Witt brothers? They are sometimes represented as a simple, clear-cut division between two political *blocs*: on the one hand, a would-be Orange dynasty supported powerfully by the broad mass of the people, strongly Calvinist ministers, still grateful for the services of the Orange heroes, William and Maurice; on the other, an oligarchy of merchant-governors representing the economic power of the thrusting economy that had arisen from the dynamic class of the Revolt itself. The Orangists are represented as standing for an aggressive kind of theocracy, straining at the leash to renew the crusade against papist Spain and her colonial empire, ready to offer slavish devotion to a central government based on the House of Orange. By contrast the States party are portrayed as almost Jeffersonian in their belief in decentralisation, minimum government, theological liberalism and consistent, if empirical, pacifism in foreign affairs.

There was a measure of truth in the contrast. The economic forces represented by the regent party were extraordinarily powerful. New, expansive capital was everywhere thrusting outwards, arrogantly rejecting the medieval restraints which Calvinism often tried to impose on it. For so far from actively promoting capitalist growth, official Calvinism was restrictive and economically antiquarian. Voetius, the ferocious doyen of the Calvinist divines of Utrecht, carried on a life-long campaign against luxury, usury, and all forms of display; excommunicating a pious woman because her husband was employed in a pawnshop, and encouraging in many other parishes a similar hostility towards anything savouring of usury or profit-making. Such fanaticism was detestable to large numbers of merchants and regents; it was not only dangerous from a material point of view, but repellent to many who were genuinely opposed on humanist grounds to persecution and bigotry of all kinds.

When the schism within Calvinism itself opened up in the early years of the century between the followers of Arminius (Remonstrants), diverging marginally on the issue of predestination from the strictly orthodox followers of Gomarus (counter-Remonstrants), the more liberal Arminians enjoyed a good measure of sympathy from the regents, though few regents openly joined the Remonstrants. C.P. Hooft, the Amsterdam regent, for example, was no Arminian. He was actively opposed to Oldenbarneveldt on many issues. Yet he (with many others) was even more bitterly opposed to the theocratic pretensions of the Gomarists. He had no intention of seeing Roman bigotry replaced by Calvinist. His ideal was a latitudinarian Protestant Church comprehending the majority of the people. His son, the poet, and Hugo Grotius, the great jurist, likewise represented a Netherlands latitudinarian tradition that was derived from Erasmus rather than from Luther or Calvin. The works of both were printed by the famous printing press of the Blaeu family, celebrated as cartographers and themselves regents.

In scores of ways, and notably as patrons of art, this ruling class demonstrated a consistently open-minded attitude in cultural affairs. Even those who were nominally Calvinists refused, when in office, to have any truck with theocratic or persecuting ideas. As a group they were culturally remarkably homogeneous. The swings from States party to Orangism and back were therefore less meaningful than they might seem to a later age. In their determination as a class to retain power, the regents were united: the conflicts that punctuated the politics of the century at intervals were often more in the nature of factious quarrels within a broadly homogeneous class than 'class struggles' of the Marxist kind. And when William III finally came back to power in 1672, even he found himself in a sense the prisoner of the regent class through whom he had to rule. Individuals might, as in 1619 and 1650, be removed, others be instated or re-instated. But the social and political dictatorship of the class went on.

The classic exposition of regent policy is to be found in the work that became known in the eighteenth century as the *Maxims* of Johan de Witt. It first appeared in 1662 under the title of *The Interest of Holland* and was in the main the work not of De Witt himself but of a prosperous Leyden clothier, Pieter de la Court. Like many of the architects of the new economy, De la Court came of a family from the South. A self-made man, his grandfather was an innkeeper from Ypres, his father an immigrant craftsman in the rejuvenated cloth industry at Leyden. De Witt read, amended and enlarged De la Court's text. The drift of the argument was pacific, mercantile, rational, anti-dynastic, a plea for economic freedom and diplomatic non-alignment.

De la Court headed his first chapter: 'Above all things war, and chiefly by sea, is most prejudicial, and peace very beneficial, for Holland'. Holland (he says) has waxed rich on *trade*. But the property of her merchants – ships, cargoes and stocks in warehouses largely – is inevitably continually at risk. It is at the mercy of the unscrupulous by land and sea. For Holland is so far in advance of others in commerce that they can take advantage of her vulnerability without real risk of reprisals. The moral is therefore plain. Under no conditions should Holland ever begin an offensive war. Her international diplomacy should be based on skilful use of the *tu quoque*. Only one power really threatens her: England. And it is not easy for the English to invade the foul and shallow waters of the Dutch coast, taking all the risks of being blown on to a lee shore by westerly winds. The right policy is not to ally with the English but

in all our differences give them good words and gain time in hopes that in these monarchical governments the kings will either follow their pleasures or through excess of luxury and court robbery, waste all their revenues and run themselves into debt or die, or perhaps fall into a foreign or intestine war.[11]

This section on Holland's international context did not merely reflect the grievous trials of the recent Anglo-Dutch war of 1652–4, from which the Dutch had emerged much the worse for wear. It also foreshadowed the almost insuperable economico-strategic problems of a small power, with lines of communication so stretched as to be almost indefensible. To such problems, he virtually admits there was no answer. Contrariwise, the economic passages are filled with optimism. Here De la Court has a consistent theme and a sovereign remedy. All will be well if Holland sticks to her convictions and retains her faith in *freedom*. To maintain and defend prosperity, and restore it when lost, freedom must be given back – to all religions, Romanist and Protestant, because

toleration and freedom of religion is not only exceedingly beneficial for our country in general but particularly for the reformed religion, which may and ought to depend on its own evidence and veracity.

Holland's prosperity had owed everything to refugees (like his own family) who had come flocking into this haven of refuge. Neither Orangist, Calvinist, nor privileged gilds and corporations, should be allowed to erode this great tradition. Taxes should be as low as possible, allowing for the need for revenue to defend Holland's shipping by strong naval forces. Tax public servants, rentiers, foreigners, even artists, but let the trader and manufacturer – the creators of prosperity – go as free as possible. Let them have their raw materials and semi-manufactured goods as cheaply as they can be obtained. And since some countries – Norway and the Baltic lands, Persia, India and China – insist on selling their goods only for coin or bullion, let the flow of precious metals be also as free as possible.

For the common people, De la Court had nothing but contempt mixed with fear. The masses, inveterate Orangists ever, must be kept in order, if necessary by force. Above all they should never be left to the leadership of the House of Orange to whom they had a superstitious and dangerous devotion: for 'where force comes, right ceaseth; and a government cannot be safe without the possession of the sword'. The Calvinist ministers, who often encouraged the rabble to oppose the excellent policies of the regents, should likewise realise their proper responsibilities and

support this free government (i.e. of the regents) and with their spiritual weapons defend it against the encroachments of such a ruler (i.e. Prince of

No society provided so amply for its poor as did
the governing merchant class of the Dutch Republic.
Homes for old people and orphans were found in every town.
Frans Hals makes of the *Lady Governors of the Old Men's Home
at Haarlem* a portrait which delineates each individual
with vivid insight. Frans Hals Museum, Haarlem.

Orange); considering that the reformed religion will be surer and better
preserved by the prudent, immortal and almost immutable sovereign
Assembly of the States of Holland and other Colleges subordinate to them,
than by those voluptuous, lavish, transitory and fickle monarchs and
princes, or their favourites, who alter the outward form and practice of
religion as may be most consistent with their pleasures and profits . . .

The *Maxims*, in short, were an all-out attack on the House of
Orange, the Calvinist Church and the people. In their confidence
in the merits of the mercantile *élite* upon whose enterprise and skill

Utility and realism were elements in the Dutch preoccupation with charity. From the outset of the Revolt, education was an important instrument of 'Protestantisation'. The Deacons' Orphanage at Amsterdam was one of the largest in Holland.

the welfare of the entire state rested they almost anticipate Alexander Hamilton; in their belief in the merits of freedom, they foreshadow Thomas Jefferson. The threat to the prosperity of Holland they diagnose as *dynasticism*, with its wild, irrational ideologies pursued to the point of war and bankruptcy. Here was the last enemy. The House of Orange seemed to the regent mind of De la Court to pose as serious a threat as the Hapsburgs had done. Centralising power would inevitably distort and destroy the basis of Dutch wealth. *A furore monarchorum, libera nos, Domine.* Here was the basic political *credo* of republican Holland. Power was a necessary ingredient of national existence: but, unlike his contemporaries, Colbert in France or George Downing in England, De la Court saw the destinies of Holland best entrusted not to an all-seeing monarch or state but to the collective enterprise of the merchant class, expanding by their own unhampered efforts. No economic *dirigisme*, no planning autocracy.

De la Court's arguments had deep roots. They represented current experience, topical problems, disagreeable memories of the recent war against England, of the recent *coup d'état* by William II in 1650 against the States party. But they derived also from ancient practice and conviction. The beliefs and aspirations were formulated more clearly and articulately, but they were essentially the same that lay behind the opposition to Alba's Tenth Penny and to Philip the Second's attempts to create a centralised, 'modern' government in the Low Countries as a whole.

Regent government was government of a kind unique in seventeenth-century Europe; a collective, social dictatorship maybe, but of a dispersed, disseminated kind, instinctively hostile to dynasticism, autocracy and theocracy alike. Smug, corrupt in places (though its ethics probably compared favourably with those of contemporary England or France), it was also benevolent and successful. Post-reformation England could also boast schools and charities financed by successful merchants; but it is doubtful if England or any other country could rival the scores of almshouses for old men and women, the orphanages, hospitals and schools maintained by private endowments from the pockets of the Dutch regent class. The economic structure they erected was in the end to prove precarious. In a world of almost continuous war, it was astonishing that it lasted as long as it did – a tribute to the flexible and ingenious policies with which the merchant governors of the Republic pursued profit and success. By and large they had every right to be proud of their achievement, to claim that the prosperity of the state was securely in their charge.

The regents, like the nobility, tended to become an hereditary caste as the century went on. Below these ruling *élites*, society broadened downwards through a series of gradations. A man's place in the middle class depended not on his having any particular occupation or profession but rather on how rich he was. Great wholesale merchants carrying on overseas or colonial trade helped to make up the upper-middle class, together with those manufacturers of cloth, or linen, or builders of ships if they employed enough hands. Below them came the professions, ministers, lawyers, professors, servants of the great companies that traded in the East and West Indies, and the majority of the middling merchants and manufacturers. Below them again, the tradesmen, farmers, skilled craftsmen, master mariners, shopkeepers and purveyors of hats, lace, cutlery and the like to the upper middle classes and their ladies. This was a stratified society but not a static one. The middle and lower-middle-class tradesmen were distinguished from their superiors as carefully as they were in contemporary France. But, as in England, success and the wealth it brought enabled many a lower-middle class tradesman to rise in the social scale.

An economy so relatively advanced depended on a large working class, skilled and unskilled. Sailors, dockside workers, net and sail makers, shipbuilding workers, cloth and linen weavers and dyers, brewers, sugar boilers, tobacco cutters and packers, farmhands in a highly commercialised and specialised agriculture – all these composed a vigorous and independent group in some ways resembling the proletariat of later industrialised societies. It was animated by a spirit of rough democracy. Even relations between masters and domestic servants were informal, as the paintings of domestic revelry by artists like Jan Steen, Ostade and others eloquently testify. Manufacturing industry was subject to periodic strikes. When workers in the Leyden cloth industry were discontented they would turn on their masters, denouncing them as blood-suckers and hinting darkly at communist solutions of their problems not unlike those being propagated in England by the Levellers.

From these social strata, Calvinism in Holland drew much of its support. Even in the earliest days of the Revolt in 1565, the mobs that destroyed statues and pictures in wild outbreaks of iconoclasm were made up of unemployed workers turned adrift in years of bad trade. This association of Calvinism with dreams of democracy and social emancipation lingered on. After the establishment of the Republic, the hold of the Calvinist ministry on the lower-middle and artisan class was, if anything, strengthened. Over them the Calvinist *predikant* exercised firm authority. With their support the Church tried to dictate to the state. Through the pyramid of committees and councils that began with the consistory or parish council and ended with Synod, the organised Calvinist Church did its best to suppress all rival creeds, whether Romanist or dissenting Protestant. This was democracy militant and utterly intolerant, the spearhead of a would-be theocracy. Its purposes and methods were alien to everything expounded in the *Maxims* of De Witt. The regents spent a good deal of the century effectively blunting the point of the Calvinist weapon.

Finally, there was a generous admixture of social dregs – the *grauw* or rabble, hated and feared by the respectable elements in society. Other countries experienced this same problem in the age of population expansion in the sixteenth century, and its social consequences continued long after the expansion had ceased. A floating mass of humanity drifted from town to town, sometimes from country to country, living on theft or violence. These were the rag-tag and bobtail, always ripe for riot and commotions. In Spain they were ready material for the picaresque novel. In Holland they offered a rich crop of subject matter for the painters who specialised in scenes of low life – the pickpockets who haunt the booths of tooth-extractors at fairs, scroungers who hang round the fringes of the *kermesse*, beggars, touts and hawkers, relics of a medieval anarchy made worse first by the demographic explosion and then by the wars: whether the problems of the *grauw* in Holland were worse than those of France, of Spain, or of England, where 'sturdy beggars' gave way to a permanent problem called collectively and simply 'the poor' (numbering maybe a quarter of the population) it is difficult to say.

With its sea ports, its open frontiers, traditions of free access and movement, the Republic, itself newly forged out of catastrophic upheaval, could scarcely avoid social problems. They were tackled brusquely and unsentimentally. The magistrates wasted no time on prison sentences, though they spent sizeable resources on 'houses of correction'. The usual medicine was the deterrent and it was exceedingly nasty. Young delinquents were branded with red-hot irons, pedlars of dirty books were dragged through the streets, or pilloried, murderers were burnt alive; the rack, whip, and torture chamber were in common use. This was brutality in an age long accustomed to brutality. The penal system reflected also a real fear of the ever-present threat of social disintegration. The merciless severity of the measures enforced by the ruling classes against disorder reflected their fear of the violence that always simmered just below the surface of this society, outwardly dedicated to those arts of peace which not only typified its own culture but powerfully influenced that of the rest of Europe also.

4 Hugo Grotius and the law of nations

The sixteenth and seventeenth centuries in Europe were a time of conscious state building, conscious growth of nationhood. The natural concomitant of these was economic expansion and economic competition. These in turn led to international friction often culminating in war. From these uneasy processes of adjustment sprang a body of rules to regulate the conduct of international relationships – rules based partly on the special interest, economic and political, of the nations which made them, partly on the general concern of all nations to introduce some measure of predictability and common standards into the conduct of international affairs. The relations of the two greatest maritime nations of Europe – Holland and Britain – were a specially fruitful source of practical rules and legal doctrines. The history of one of these doctrines – that of the freedom of the seas – was of fundamental importance. Let us look forward to the nineteenth century for an authoritative statement of it – to 1817, when Lord Stowell gave it as his opinion that 'All nations being equal, all have an equal right to the uninterrupted use of the unappropriated parts of the ocean for their navigation.'

This signified the burial, long overdue, of a doctrine of maritime sovereignty which had been dead for a hundred years and moribund for fifty before that, and its official replacement by the doctrine of the freedom of the seas.

During the nineteenth century this doctrine came to be regarded as specially a British conception, bound up indissolubly with the spread of British dominion over the map of the world. In fact, the doctrine of the freedom of the seas – the doctrine that every nation has equal rights of navigation and fishing on the high seas – was a Dutch doctrine, the work of the great Dutch jurist, Hugo Grotius, who in the early seventeenth century preached it on behalf of his seafaring nation in flat defiance of the other three important maritime powers, Spain, Portugal – and Britain herself. For in spite of all that has been written and said about the spacious days of Queen Elizabeth, Jacobean England was still parochially-minded, with a sea-borne trade that was only just beginning to stretch its sea-legs; militarily, Britain was on the defensive, and her ideas on international usage lagged a long way behind the bold but intermittent voyages of Elizabeth's chartered pirates.

Much has been written about Grotius, 'the founder of modern international law', but it has not always been clear how essential was the relationship between Grotius's ideas and the practical needs of the Dutch merchants and seagoing traders of his time, nor how it came about that a doctrine which suited the Dutch in one century came to suit the British in the next. Grotius's opinions on international law were neither academic nor wholly altruistic, though neither were they venal or purely nationalist. They were largely conditioned by the economic system under which the Dutch traded and became a wealthy colonial power. In particular, his doctrine of the freedom of the seas reflects the interest of Dutch shipping and trade in 1600 as accurately as the later British doctrine of the right of search reflected the needs of British naval strategy. That Grotius's writings give the impression of being written *sub specie aeternitatis* is partly because, being a good lawyer, he chose his examples and proofs from the safe distance of classical antiquity, avoiding the thornier paths of contemporary events. Grotius was neither academic nor transcendental. He was a man of great energy, practical and versatile, a practising lawyer, a great classical scholar, a poet and philologist, a theologian, an administrator, a politician and diplomat.

During the twelve years truce with Spain, Oldenbarneveldt, Grand Pensionary of Holland, appointed Grotius Pensionary of Rotterdam. Later he visited England to help in settling disputes which had arisen between the English and Dutch East India Companies. It was partly these contacts with England which led him

RUIT HORA

Hugo *Grotius*

See you not Learning in his Lookes?
See it more Lively in his Bookes.

Hugo de Groot (Grotius), polymath and humanist, was the brain of the States party, and is justly regarded as the founder of modern international law.

into serious troubles at home. In Holland the great dispute was raging between the orthodox Calvinists (the predestinarians or Contra-Remonstrants) led by Gomarus, and the Remonstrants, led by Arminius, who wanted to soften the rigours of predestinarian orthodoxy. Grotius, a tolerant and reasonable man in an age which generally favoured neither tolerance nor reason, inclined to the views of Arminius and supported him in discussions with James I and the Archbishop of Canterbury. As a result of these discussions, Grotius drafted a resolution calling a conference to settle the religious disputes in the Netherlands and empowering the Dutch municipalities to set up militia to maintain civil order. Grotius had the misfortune to belong by temperament and conviction to the wrong side – the side which was doomed to defeat at the Synod of Dort. He was imprisoned along with Oldenbarneveldt, but escaped his fate of execution. Everyone knows the story of his escape from the prison at the castle of Loevestein in a trunk – a tale worthy of Dumas: from there he escaped to Antwerp and Paris. His later days were spent in the diplomatic service of Sweden.

Grotius was one of the thinkers who both represented and created the outlook and policy of the States party. His views on politics and religion were typical of the liberal-minded regent, Erasmian and in the true tradition of humanism. Prince Maurice of Orange showed his usual shrewd appreciation of the situation when he arrested him along with the leader of the regent party, Oldenbarneveldt; for if Oldenbarneveldt was the hand, Grotius was the brain of the anti-Orange party. His legal genius he placed at the disposal of his fellow regents. As a regent he believed firmly and genuinely in the mission of the merchant governors of Holland to shape the spiritual as well as the material welfare of the new Republic. He had no problem in reconciling his conscience with the needs of his country's trade. Here (as with De la Court) the idea of 'freedom' is beginning to acquire a moral colouring which justifies its practical utility.

To understand how revolutionary Grotius's doctrines were, we need only examine briefly his contemporaries' idea on maritime rights. The sixteenth century was an age of 'closed waters', when states were in the habit of claiming absolute sovereignty over their local seas. Venice claimed sovereignty over the Adriatic; Britain claimed to rule the seas which surrounded the British Isles, while Denmark and Sweden disputed rule in the Baltic. Even the advent of longer overseas voyages did not by any means spell the end of the old theory. The great colonial powers of the sixteenth century, Spain and Portugal, continued to apply it to their overseas possessions, the Spaniards claiming the Pacific and the Gulf of Mexico, Portugal the south Atlantic and the Indian Ocean, basing their claims partly on conquest, partly on discovery and occupation and partly on papal award. Foreigners were therefore excluded from these waters. It was the intrusion of the Dutch, thrusting south to Africa and eastwards to Mauritius, then to Java and Moluccas, which put an end to the old ideas: the test came in 1602, when a Dutch ship belonging to the East Indies Company captured a Portuguese galleon, the *Catherine*, in the Malacca Straits. Grotius was retained as counsel for the East Indies Company, and was largely responsible for securing the forfeit and confiscation of the goods aboard the galleon in the Amsterdam Court of Admiralty.

During the negotiations which led to the twelve years truce with Spain, the Spaniards tried to persuade the Dutch to renounce their claims to trade in the East and West Indies. It was then, in 1608, that Grotius expanded and published his earlier brief under the title *The Freedom of the Seas or the Right that Belongs to the Dutch to take part in the East Indian Trade*. What was not known until 1868 was that this was only an isolated chapter of a much greater work – the *De Jure Praedae* – (*Concerning the Law of Prize*).

In the *Mare Liberum*. Grotius was mainly concerned to refute the Spanish and Portuguese claims to sovereignty over those tropical seas into which his countrymen were penetrating, but his denial carried with it implications which were designed to alter the whole theory of maritime rights – and amongst those affected the British were not the least concerned. Grotius sets out the quarrel succinctly:

Between us and the Spaniards the following points are in dispute: Can the vast, the boundless sea be the appanage of one Kingdom alone, and it not the greatest? Can any one Nation have the right to prevent other nations which so desire from selling to one another, from bartering with one another, actually from communicating with one another? Can any Nation give away what it never owned, or discover what already belonged to someone else? Does a manifest injustice of long standing create a specific right?[12]

He then proceeds to show that the Portuguese have no right to sovereignty over the East Indies either by discovery, by war, by occupation or by papal donation. Therefore, he continues:

... freedom of trade is based on a primitive right of Nations which has a natural and permanent cause; and so that right cannot be destroyed, or at all events it may not be destroyed, except by the consent of all Nations.

Nevertheless, if the United Provinces were to be driven into war by the injustice of their enemies, the justice of their cause would give them hope and confidence in the final outcome:

Therefore, if it be necessary, Arise, O Nation unconquered on the sea, and fight boldly, not only for your own liberation but for that of the human race. Nor let it fright thee that their fleet is winged, each ship with an hundred oars. The sea whereon it sails will have none of it. And though the prows bear figures threatening to cast rocks such as Centaurs throw, thou shalt find them but hollow planks and painted terrors. 'Tis his cause that makes or mars a soldier's strength. If the cause be not just, shame strikes the weapon from his hands.

So far as colonial trade was concerned, the British vested interests were as yet not extensive, though, as we have seen, Grotius was sent to England to help mediate in minor disputes. There was, however, a fruitful field of controversy and dissension nearer home – the fisheries off the English and Scottish coasts which were largely exploited by Dutch fishermen.

Few examples of Dutch economic and technological superiority were so galling to the seventeenth century Englishman as the hold which these rivals had acquired over the rich fishing grounds along the east coast of England and Scotland. Every year saw its triumphal parade and demonstration. The herring fishery of the Dutch along the British coast was known in the Republic as the *Groote Visscherij* (Great Fishery) as distinct from the local fresh-herring fisheries. Minutely regulated by the 'College of the Fishery', to which only five Dutch ports were admitted, it formed a vital element

in the trade, employment, and export business of the Republic. The Dutch 'busses' collected at Bressay Sound in Shetland early in June every year. The solemn opening of the season was fixed at St John's Day (24 June). Guarded by warships, the fishing fleet moved steadily southward. Until St James's Day (25 July) it was limited to the Isles and down to Buchan Ness. Thence, till Elevation Day (14 September) it moved to the Northumberland coast; then, till St Catherine's Day (25 September) to the deep waters off Yarmouth; and so to the Thames mouth early in December. The herrings were caught overnight, salted, barrelled, and preserved by the old method invented by Beukelsz, a Zeelander, in the late fifteenth century and transported to Holland. Then they were repacked, branded and exported. They formed a valuable addition to export cargoes not only to the Catholic south of Europe, but to the Baltic (where the local herring fishery had declined and in some cases disappeared in the previous century). The value of the total Dutch catch was estimated at anything from one to three million sterling. A conservative estimate of two million pounds would put its national economic value at something roughly equivalent to the total export value of Britain's famous cloth industry.

As a source of direct employment, the herring fishing was equally important. About 37,000 fishermen were employed, 32,000 in the herring fishing, another 5,000 in the associated Dogger Bank fisheries that caught cod and ling. Indirectly, the value was much greater. For the fisheries created a demand for ships, sails, nets, barrels, salt, provisions and the like. It was, in fact, what a twentieth-century economist might call a multiplier, creating a network of related demands throughout Holland's economy. This, the Dutch boasted, was their 'gold mine'. The English were only too ready to agree. But the 'gold mine' gave rise to ugly incidents. Grotius found himself having to apologise for the ill-manners of Dutch fishermen who landed on the Scottish and English coasts, misbehaving, polluting churches and pulpits, stealing poultry and eggs, shooting at native fishermen and (on one occasion) holding upside down an honest young woman selling stockings, a disagreeable experience from which she was somewhat improbably alleged to have later died. Such outrages, real, imagined, or exaggerated, caused much resentment and heart-searching. Petitions slowly percolated through the creaking machinery of government to the Privy Council and became great occasions of state representation. Successive English governments attempted to restrict or prohibit the Dutch fishermen.

Grotius played a prominent part in the discussions that ensued between the governments of England and the Republic. His principles were consistent. The fisheries, like navigation and trade, ought to remain 'free and open to all'. But in the strained atmosphere of English constitutional affairs, his further remarks on the right to levy revenue could hardly be regarded by the Parliamentarians as doing anything but adding insult to injury:

Similarly, revenues levied on maritime fisheries are held to belong to the Crown, but they do not bind the sea itself or the fisheries, but only the persons engaged in fishing. Wherefore subjects for whom a state or ruler is by common consent competent to make laws, will perhaps be compelled to bear such charges, but so far as other persons are concerned, the right of fishing ought everywhere to be exempt from tolls, lest a servitude be imposed upon the sea, which is not susceptible to a servitude.

In other words, James I might tax English fishermen, but not Dutch.

The implications of Grotius's theory did not go unnoticed in England where Selden produced his *Mare Clausum* to defend the old theory and especially to refute Grotius's claims for the Dutch fishermen. (Selden's work was written in 1617 but not published until 1635.) Selden's thesis was twofold: first,

that the sea, by the law of nature or nations, is not common to all men, but capable of private dominion or property as well as the land;

and secondly,

that the King of Great Britain is Lord of the sea flowing about, as an inseparable appendant of the British Empire.[13]

Since the Scottish fisheries were likewise in bondage to the Dutch, we find William Welwood, a lawyer of Aberdeen University, expressing views similar to Selden's in his *Abridgement of all the Sea-Lawes* (1613).

What was the result of this conflict between the new theory and the old? It was, briefly, that for some years the English won a victory for the old theory of maritime sovereignty. They compelled the Dutch to take out English licences to fish off the English coasts. In 1636 the Dutch tried to ignore the demand and fish without a license: they were attacked and compelled to pay £30,000 for leave to remain. On the whole the British succeeded in enforcing their sovereignty by making the Dutch accord honours of the flag (symbolising maritime sovereignty). The Dutch had to acknowledge the obligation in the two treaties of Westminster (1654 and 1674) and in the Treaty of Breda in 1667. But the conflict had already largely lost its point, and towards the end of the century events moved rapidly. By 1667 a turning point had been reached in Anglo-Dutch relations; the colonial disputes were largely settled, and the way was clear for an alliance which began in 1689 and lasted for two generations, first under William III and then under Marlborough and Heinsius.

By 1700 the old theory of maritime sovereignty was dwindling away as British ocean-going trade extended as widely as the Dutch trade had done a century earlier. British fishing vessels were roaming as far into foreign waters as the Dutch, and the old parochialism was outmoded. The doctrine of freedom of the seas was a doctrine appropriate to an expanding national economy: as Britain, learning from the Dutch, came to contest the Dutch monopoly of world trade and passed to an economic offensive against the vested economic rights of the other powers, it became expedient for Britain to take over the Dutch doctrine of the *mare liberum*.

By the time Grotius's name was fully restored to honour in his own country, his theory, devised to justify and extend his own nations's commerce and navigation, had been appropriated by another power, and the Dutch were shaping for a neutral or at most passive role in European politics. In the eighteenth century one of the most powerful factors which shaped the development of international law was the jostling of the Dutch by the main belligerent powers, Britain and France. Under this stimulus the Dutch – principally the great jurist, Van Bijnkershoek – built upon Grotius's foundations a whole theory of the laws of neutrality. In a problem which was a brutally practical one, theory was not of much assistance. Grotius in his *De Jure Belli ac Pacis* had merely commented that the duty of a neutral was not to help a belligerent carrying on an unjust war, nor to hinder a belligerent carrying on a just war: and in doubtful cases 'to act alike to both sides, in permitting transit, in shipping provisions to the respective armies, and in not assisting persons besieged.' In translating this into practice, the main problems to be solved were: first, what goods might Dutch ships supply to a belligerent and secondly (since the Dutch were a great carrying power), what belligerent goods might be carried in neutral bottoms? As regards contraband, Grotius's analysis remained; goods were classed as (a) objects of use in war only; (b) goods useless in war, such as luxury articles; (c) money, provisions, ships, etc., which were useful in peace and war. But as to definition, opinions differed, as they have always continued to differ, and practice varied according to requirements and convenience. Not unnaturally, Van Bijnkershoek devoted his efforts to limiting the range of prohibited articles.

In the matter of the carriage of enemy goods, Grotius had held to the old theory that all enemy goods were liable to seizure. But after the middle of the seventeenth century, the Dutch evolved the doctrine of 'free ships, free goods' which went to the opposite extreme. Between 1650 and 1700 they persuaded Spain, Portugal, France, and Sweden to grant the privilege in no fewer than twelve treaties. Britain never regarded herself as bound by these; she went on seizing enemy goods while releasing the ships with payment of freight – a policy which brought her into collision with the neutrals in 1780, when the first Armed Neutrality put forward the immunity of belligerent cargoes in neutral ships as one of its main doctrines. A Dutch convoy was captured and taken into Spithead. Dutch protests were answered with the threat that all foreign vessels found assisting the enemy with warlike stores might be considered lawful prize. The last Anglo-Dutch War broke out in December 1780.

The men of the seventeenth century mostly believed firmly in the merits of property and the sense of political and social responsibility that the ownership of property conferred. Ideas of law reflected

Serenissime ac Potentissime Rex
Domine clementissime.

190

Quo magis constet de amico gratoqᵉ animo clementissimæ Reginæ Meæ rectorumqᵉ Regni Sueciæ pro hactenus præstito amico affectu ac beneuolentiâ, ac Meæ garᵉ pro Majestatis Vestræ in Meᵃ fauentᵉ benignitate, utᵒ magis ac magis æstatis detur, Eidem Vestræ Majestati perstandi in tam amicâ ac benignâ voluntate, eᵗ eᵒ existimari Legatum Suæ Regiæ Majestatis Reginæ Meæ Regniqᵉ nomine ex potestate Mihi concessâ mittere Magnificum, et Nobilem Dᵑᵘᵐ Hugonem Grotium, dictæ Suæ Regᵉ Majᵗⁱˢ Consiliarium, quem multas ob causas acceptum fore Regᵉ Majᵗⁱˢ Præ confido eoqᵉ ut ei tanquam Mihi aut ipsis Regni Sueciæ rectoribus fidem tribeat Majestas, amicoqᵉ in Reginam, Regnumqᵉ Sueciæ animo, in Me beneuolentᵉ audiat ea quæ nomine Nostro dicturus sit, eᵗ quæ pro Eorum temporum ratione ostendenda tribuit Vᵃᵉ Majestati. Illud Spondere possum, clementissimæ Meæ Reginæ, rectoribus, Regnoqᵉ Sueciæ nunquam defore gratum Mihiqᵉ addictum, eᵗ sequentem, in Majestatem Vram animum, neqᵉ prætermissuras ullas abire occasiones quibus id demonstrari possit. Quas ego Ieclandᵒ DEM precor Rex Potentissime, ut paternâ curâ tueatur vitam, incolumitatem, ac salutem Vestræ Majestatis, quippe qui sim, tribeaqᵉ semper cupiam

Sᵃᵉ Regiæ Majestatis Vestræ

Datum Moguntiaci
die XXVII Decembris
Anno M.DC.XXXIV

Humillimus et obligantissimus servitor
Axelius
Oxenstierna

In 1634 the Swedish Chancellor, Oxenstierna,
appointed Grotius as Swedish ambassador to France
with this letter to King Louis XIII.

71

this belief. International law, as much as domestic laws, embodied the same anxiety of the acquisitive to protect what they have acquired or what they hope to acquire. Grotius presents a case on behalf of the hopeful and expansive merchant adventurers of the Republic. It is somewhat analogous to the change that had come about in England. Here land had ceased to be the basis of public law. Words like 'liberty' and 'freedom', once attached to rights of specific pieces of property, were being transmuted into more general rights available if not to all, at any rate to a growing circle of citizens as the world understood the term.

Grotius was in some measure doing for international law what Locke was to do for English public and private law. Least of all would it be sensible to seek in this republic of merchants, particularly in the thought of the philosopher and legal oracle of the regent class, any admission that trade was tainted or unworthy. For the citizens of Holland, the economy and society of the Republic was a natural evolution of the traditional Netherlands way of life. Invention, ingenuity and enterprise had placed them a long way ahead of the rest of Europe in wealth. Merchants and bankers had not loaded the people with debt as medieval usurers had burdened the peasant farmers. They did not bring the squalor or misery that was to be associated with industry in a later age. This was the most urbanised corner of Europe, but it was unbelievably swept and garnished, and its people enjoyed generally high living standards. Its merchants had profited by the needs of the rest of Europe but they had at any rate supplied them – corn, salt, fish, spices, silks, cloths, tea, coffee, tobacco, rice, were a few of the common products they carried, stored and sold.

This was a callous age. The servants of the great trading companies did not always respect the orders of their superiors thousands of miles away in Holland. Grotius was defending a body of commercial interests, legitimate but by no means spotless. Yet both he and De la Court were pointing in the direction that events were to follow. Behind the spreading Dutch economy of their day were energies making for economic growth, and these demanded freedom to develop. Their common theme was that economic freedom was necessary and justified. This was the contribution that the Dutch economy in its phase of expansion made to economic ideology. There was always a party fighting not only against the exclusiveness of Spain, Portugal and England, but against the forces of monopoly and intolerance at home. Empirical and self-interested though they were, these ideas were transmitted down through the next century to become part of the *laissez-faire* philosophy. In Grotius, the same fundamental belief in freedom transmuted what might have been simply special pleading into something more noble and enduring. In his introduction to his great *De Jure Belli ac Pacis* Grotius wrote:

A citizen who conducts himself in accordance with the laws of his country does not thereby behave foolishly, although, in consequence of these laws, he must deny himself certain things which might be of advantage to him personally. Similarly, a nation cannot reasonably be considered foolish that does not so strongly emphasise its own interests as to tread under foot the common laws of States and Nations. The cases are identical, for a citizen who for his direct advantage infringes the social laws of his country destroys the foundations of his higher interests and at the same time those of his descendants. The nation that opposes the law of nature and the law of nations overthrows the bulwark of its future peace.

In the *Mare Liberum* we have seen Grotius justifying the right of an offended nation to wage war; not that, in an age which took for granted the unrestrained right of waging war, many would have been found to quibble over that. The novelty in Grotius's doctrines was that they attacked that unrestrained right and limited it strictly to an instrument for use against 'guilty' states. Like the founders of the League of Nations, Grotius wanted a world

Court of Justice; with characteristically practical wisdom he recommended also that it should have executive powers to carry out its sentences. In Holland his attempts to reconcile the Calvinists and the extreme Arminians like Episcopius met with little success. Yet in Scotland his *De Veritate Religione Christianae*, the *De Satisfactione Christi* and his commentaries on various books of the Bible, were reading common to Episcopalians and Presbyterians alike; and while some of the latter regarded him as 'Tridentine poperie' and some of the former thought him a Socinian, both sides acknowledged his eminence. Slowly the leaven of his reasonableness worked and the comparative tolerance of the eighteenth century owed much to him. Samuel Johnson took great comfort from Grotius's steady Christian faith:

Grotius [he said] was not a recluse, but a man of the world who certainly had no bias to the side of religion. Grotius was an acute man, a lawyer, a man accustomed to examine evidence, and he was convinced.[14]

And in 1777 Johnson recommended to the Archbishop of Canterbury as a candidate for entrance to the Charterhouse one De Groot, a man 'old, poor and infirm in a great degree.' But he had another claim 'to which no scholar can refuse attention.' He was:

. . . by several descents the nephew of Hugo Grotius; of him from whom perhaps every man of learning has learnt something. Let it not be said [concludes Johnson's letter to the Rector of Lambeth] that in any lettered country a nephew of Grotius asked a charity and was refused.[15]

To the Archbishop's credit, let it be said that it was not.

5 An expanding world economy

Along the lines of the expanding network of world trade that centred on Amsterdam from 1600 onwards flowed capital, technical skill and people. Just as in the nineteenth century Britain helped to transform the world by exporting capital and skill, so in the seventeenth Holland helped to illuminate and develop many obscure and backward corners of Europe. Though inevitably the rate of change was much smaller and slower, it was not negligible. By its economic and technological rationality and modernity, the Dutch Republic influenced many countries. Throughout western Europe, and further afield too, colonies of Dutch merchants, engineers, artisans, could be found at work. What the ubiquitous Scottish engineer was to the nineteenth century, his Dutch predecessor was to the seventeenth. These colonies of emigrant Dutch, and the local capital investments with which they were often associated, grew out of the ordinary processes of trade which had given Dutch merchants a stake in this area or that. The need to manage or invest capital surpluses arising out of trade drew men after their money.

Traditionally, long before the Revolt or the Republic, the Baltic trade had formed the backbone of the trading system built up by the northern Netherlanders. In the late sixteenth century the Dutch ships loaded with Baltic grain penetrated to the eastern Mediterranean. The Dutch traders thus became a permanent link between north and south Europe. By the seventeenth century Scandinavia and northern Europe were prominent as areas of investment and settlement for Dutch capitalists and skilled workmen. Gothenburg was planned and laid out by Dutch engineers with canals and sluices in the Dutch style. Five of the twelve members of its first town council were Dutch. The port and fishery and a tar company were run by Dutch settlers. The Gothenburg sick were tended by Dutch doctors and Gothenburg babies delivered by a Dutch midwife.

Huet, Bishop of Avranches, wrote in his *Memoirs* of the Dutch trade (1694):

It may be said that the Dutch are in some respects masters of the commerce of the Swedish Kingdom since they are masters of the copper trade. The farmers of these mines, being always in need of money, and not finding any in Sweden, pledge this commodity to merchants of Amsterdam who advance them the necessary funds. It is the same with tar and pitch, certain merchants of Amsterdam having bought the greater part of these farms of the King, and made considerable advances besides, so that the result is that these commodities and most others are found as cheap in Amsterdam as in Sweden.[16]

The most spectacular operators were Louis de Geer and Elias Trip (the latter of a family that inspired one of the finest portraits by Rembrandt). Both families came, like many leading entrepreneurs in the early history of the Republic, from what is now Belgium. *Liègois*, they were experts in the metallurgy and armament manufacture that characterised their native city. As Huet explained, their role was to provide the scarce capital and skill by which the rich copper and iron deposits of Sweden could fructify. Through these advances the Dutch concessionaires became deeply involved in the public finances of the Swedish monarchy. In 1618 De Geer, with a consortium of other Amsterdam merchants, made himself responsible for the payment by Gustavus Adolphus of the interest and capital in respect of a large loan by the States General for the ransom of the fortress of Elfsborg from the Danes.

The loan of 1618 was the start of a long chapter of enterprise by De Geer in Sweden. Mining concessions were its original centre, but by the mid century they were only part of a network of enterprises that included timber concessions, foundries, sawmills, warehouses, factories, as well as wholesale and retail stores where the De Geer daughters sold pots, pans and cutlery over the counter. Advances were made on the security of mining resources and taxes

An example of Dutch influence on English architecture: Bourne Pond Mill, Colchester, home of a flourishing Dutch cloth industry, with characteristic gables in Netherlands style.

to the government. In 1645 he assembled, chartered and equipped a Swedish fleet against Denmark. It cost (he claimed) nearly a million and a half guilders. Eventually De Geer was naturalised and ennobled by the Vasas, though he continued to live half his life in Amsterdam. His partner and sometime rival, Trip, similarly became a copper concessionaire and monopolist, a substantial creditor of the Swedish Crown. By the 1630s he calculated his claims at nearly a million guilders and in 1682 his heirs were still lamenting that they were owed 'many hundred thousand guilders'. Like the Jewish and Italian bankers before them, these Dutch merchant bankers found that a long spoon was necessary if they were to sup with royalty.

As the struggle for power in the Baltic developed, Sweden moved out of the Dutch orbit and Denmark moved in. Here the Marselis family (like the Trips and De Geers, of south Netherlands origin) functioned in much the same way as their rivals in Sweden, mining, exporting timber and munitions and acting as government contractors and financiers. In 1645, while De Geer was fitting out his squadron for the Swedes, Marselis was doing the same for the Danes. Like the De Geers, the Marselis became the owners of great estates in Denmark and Norway.

In Norway (part of the Danish kingdom) there were other Dutch rivals. The copper mines here (the French economist Savary wrote in 1675)

belong in part to the estate of the treasurer of the King of Denmark, and to two merchants of Amsterdam who ordinarily market the product in Amsterdam or London.[17]

One was Joachim Irgens, who had settled in Amsterdam in 1652 from Holstein and married into the princely Bicker family, themselves closely connected with the Grand Pensionary De Witt. By the 1650s Irgens was advancing large sums of his own to the

Danish King on the security of copper mines and acting as the funnel by which the savings of scores of small Dutch investors found their way to Norway. He too ended as a landed proprietor in Denmark and Norway.

There were numerous other smaller entrepreneurs. William Davidson, a Scot long settled in Amsterdam, owned a third of the capital of a Danish salt company. The brothers Sautijn jointly mined and exported sulphur from Iceland. These were no mere speculators and financiers. They undertook all the extraction, manufacturing and commercial processes necessary to their enterprises, as well as raising the capital. Dutch immigrant entrepreneurs dominated the economic life of Scandinavia and Iceland, where they fished for everything from salmon to great whales and hunted the great Icelandic falcon much prized by wealthy sportsmen throughout Europe.

In Russia a small group of Amsterdammers monopolised the export of caviare and isinglass (possibly a corruption of the Dutch *huisenbles*), tar, hemp, oil, salmon and wool. In Poland they

From the sixteenth century, Dutch engineers were at work on projects to drain the marshy Tuscan coastal plain from Leghorn and Pisa southwards as far as Rome, and to provide canal transport from cities like Florence and Rome to the sea. This plan is from a book by Cornelius Meyer (1678) describing his scheme for Rome. The economic attractions of such projects lay mainly in the opportunities for cheap transport of grain, wine, and other bulky freight.

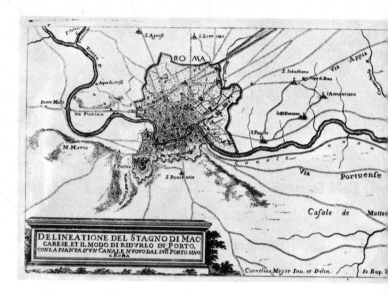

organised and operated the Mint. Wherever Dutch capitalists went in the north they were to be found draining swamps, clearing forests, building canals, opening mines, building ships, mills, factories for gunpowder, glass, textiles. Thus Amsterdam capital reached out into Europe's backward areas, fertilising and fructifying as it went.

In south or Latin Europe, the Dutch were also prominent as merchants but there was less permanent settlement or investment. Dutch merchants lent to the Venetian republic. Dutch engineers were employed by the Duke of Tuscany to drain the Tuscan marshes and canalise rivers. A Dutch syndicate acquired a monopoly of Italian marble export that explained why there were 'the vast magazines of Amsterdam . . . that a man would think . . . there were Quarries of Marble near the City Gates', why the great

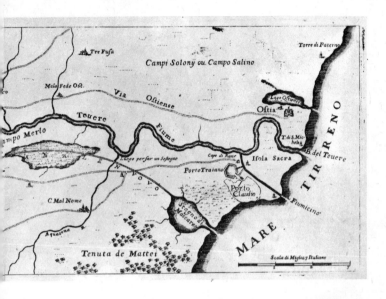

Overleaf: This map shows principal West European hydraulic engineering projects carried out or supervised by the Dutch during seven centuries. In Holland itself, almost two million acres have been dredged or reclaimed since records began.

merchant houses along the Amsterdam canals are still lined with marble, and why the marble for Versailles was purchased there. In the Habsburg Empire, the government conceded the quicksilver deposits of Idria and the copper mines of Hungary to the banking house of Deutz in Amsterdam in much the same fashion as the Swedish Vasas had conceded their metal resources to the Trips and De Geers.

Even France, though more developed than the northern countries, offered a fruitful field for Dutch enterprise. Most characteristic was the *Société pour le Desséchement des Marais et Lacs de France*, a project engineered by Humphrey Bradley, who, despite his English-sounding name, was a Brabanter. (An earlier offer by Bradley to allow Queen Elizabeth to share the benefits of a similar scheme in England had been rejected. Now he turned his

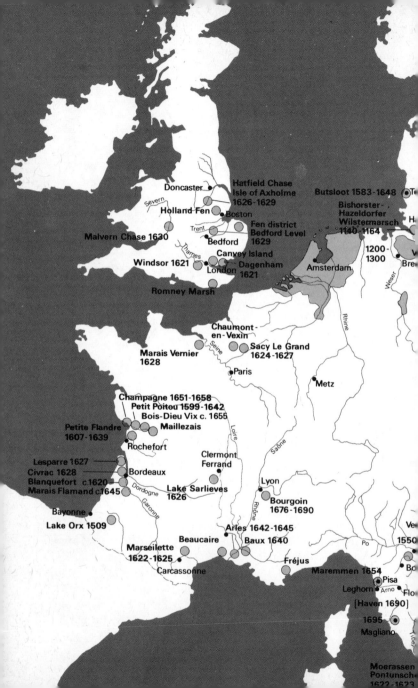

Doncaster

Hatfield Chase
Isle of Axholme
1626-1629

Butsloot 1583-1648

Bishorster -
Hazeldorfer
Wilstermarsch
1140-1164

Severn

Holland Fen

Boston

Trent

Fen district
Bedford Level
1629

1200-
1300

Malvern Chase 1630

Bedford

Bre

Windsor 1621

Canvey Island

Dagenham
1621

London

Amsterdam

Weser

Romney Marsh

Rhine

Chaumont -
en-Vexin

Marais Vernier
1628

Seine

Sacy Le Grand
1624-1627

Paris

Metz

Champagne 1651-1658
Petit Poitou 1599-1642
Bois-Dieu Vix c. 1655

Loire

Saône

Maillezais

Petite Flandre
1607-1639

Rochefort

Clermont
Ferrand

Lyon

Lesparre 1627
Civrac 1628
Blanquefort c.1620
Marais Flamand c1645

Bordeaux

Dordogne

Lake Sarlieves
1626

Rhône

Bourgoin
1676-1690

Garonne

Bayonne

Lake Orx 1509

Arles 1642-1645

Baux 1640

Ve

Po

1550

Beaucaire

Marseilette
1622-1625

Carcassonne

Fréjus

Maremmen 1654

Bo

Pisa

Leghorn

Arno

Flo

[Haven 1690]

1695

Magliano

Moerassen
Pontunsch
1622-1623

1640

Gothenburg
1610-1620

Amager 1600

c.1700

Elbing c.1700
Danzig Prussian Holland 1297
Tiegenhof 1528-1562

Stettin
walde 1500-1600
Neuholland Friedeberg
Oranienburg 1600-1700 1603
Berlin Ciechocinek Torun
600-1700 1700-1800 1600-1700
1700-1800 Warsaw
Lodz Saska Kepa 1624
Kozienice

Netze

Vistula

Oder

Spree

Warthe

Pilica

Narew

Bug

1700-1800

1599

Ostrog

Slobodskie Hollendry
1800-1825

our c.1690)

o

attention to France.) In a number of provinces groups of Dutch entrepreneurs undertook ambitious drainage schemes financed by Jan Hoeufft, whose firm was later to be a major source of credit and armaments for Richelieu.

The French *Société* was both topical and prophetic. In France as in England these were times when the monarchy, hard hit by inflation, was desperately searching for any unexploited assets to bridge the gap between income and expenditure. The idea of realising the value of marshes and fens was seductive to large landowners as well.

From 1599, an edict named Bradley Master of the Dykes of the Kingdom, and decreed that 'all the fens and marshes . . . should be dried out and cleaned up by the said Bradley and his associates, or by the owners, and made by them suitable for working for the plough, or as fields or pasture . . .'. Not only were the participants Dutch or Flemish – the Comans (Coymans), les Vanuppe (van Uppe), the De la Planche; the company also got permission 'to build houses, townships and villages to house and draw in a number of Flemish, Dutch and other foreign families'. This settlement left permanent traces in French place names – the Petite-Flandre in Saintonge, the Polder of Holland in the Médoc area, and the names of farms, like La Haye in Vendée. In 1607, legal documents were drawn up for the *Société* and the privileges were renewed in 1639, on the death of the chief engineer, in favour of his fellow citizens, since close family ties unified these immigrants, who shared work of this kind throughout the kingdom. The Franco-Dutch wars, and the revocation of the Edict of Nantes created difficulties. Some of the operators were thrown into prison and goods were seized. All this failed to prevent the work from continuing. The drainage of the marshlands of Guienne and Vexin, those of Languedoc and Provence, as far as the lake of Sarlière in Auvergne and the marshlands of the Dauphiné, was added to the work on the marshes of Poitou and Saintonge. All these areas benefited from the care of these experienced engineers who brought vast areas of land under cultivation.

Many other industries owe their acclimatisation in France to the Dutch. Established in ports such as Rouen, Nantes, La Rochelle, Bordeaux and Marseilles, sometimes from as far back as the fourteenth century, and maintaining quite sizeable communities in some of the ports, they did not confine themselves to maritime and commercial activities only. In Nantes they had a monopoly of the wine trade, buying the harvest in the field from the owners and thus creating agricultural credit. In Rouen they owned a brewery, in Angers and Saumur sugar-refining factories and paper-mills in Angoumois. Colbert favoured the establishment of the Van Robais clothiers in Abbeville. The Van Robais had come from Middelburg: others established themselves at Louviers.

They were no less interested in naval construction, a science in which they had no equal in Europe. Colbert sent Dutch carpenters to Brest, Toulon, Marseilles and La Rochelle. These were the engineers who built the locks of the Midi Canal and it is therefore not surprising that there are so many Dutch words in French navigational terms – words such as *fret, lest, flute, yacht, quille, babord* and *tribord, ecope, pompe*, and, if not *godiller*, then surely *godailler*, is also a marine word.

For centuries the Dutch had made themselves masters of the science of drainage. Large areas of Holland and Zeeland were reclaimed from the sea. The fact was a source of sour amusement to the English. A land below sea-level! Andrew Marvell in his *Character of Holland* (1665) set to work to do satirical justice to a country where

> The fish oft times the burger dispossest
> And sat, not as a meat, but as a guest.

Sour grapes? England was still apprenticed to the Dutch not only

An engine, the water pump made by Pieter Mauritz (Peter Morice) in 1582 as part of his scheme to supply water to Londoners.

in matters of trade, finance, printing, science, architecture and painting, but in engineering itself. Many English engineering and reclamation works of this period were carried out by Dutch technicians. The first successful project (1582) for supplying London with drinking water was carried out by Peter Morice, a Dutchman, who erected a pumping engine in the first arch of London Bridge, worked by water wheels which forced the water through lead pipes into the houses. The force of water was such that Morice was able to throw water 'over St Magnus's steeple, greatly to the astonishment of the Mayor and Aldermen, who assembled to witness the experiment.' A little later Johannes Croppenburgh and a company of Dutch workmen were reclaiming and embanking Canvey Island near the mouth of the Thames, while Cornelius Vandervelt enclosed Wapping Marsh by means of a high bank along which the present High Street was made. At Yarmouth, Jansen, another Dutchman, was employed to construct the new harbour, while the enclosure of Brading Haven in the Isle of Wight was carried out by Sir Hugh Myddelton in 1620 with the aid of 'Dutchmen brought out of the Low Countries'.

It was in connection with the repair of a breach in the Thames Embankment at Dagenham in 1621 that we first hear of the greatest of the Dutch immigrant engineers, Cornelius Vermuyden. Vermuyden was a native of Zeeland and an experienced embanking engineer. The success of his operations at Dagenham led to a contract to drain the Royal Park at Windsor. There he became known to Charles I who shortly after employed him on the first of the two great projects which occupied the rest of his life, brought him fame and notoriety, ruined his health and finally brought him in old age to poverty and disappointment: this was the drainage of Hatfield Chase on the borders of Yorkshire.

His second project for the drainage of the Lincoln and Cambridge Fens was even more ambitious. The contract for the drainage of the

Chase was drawn up on 24 May 1626, Vermuyden undertaking to make the drowned lands fit for tillage and pasturage. In return he was to have one third of the reclaimed land. The 'adventure' was financed by a company composed chiefly of Dutch capitalists – Mathew Valkenburgh, the Van Peenens, John Corsellis and others. The workmen were also mainly Dutch or Flemish, drawn from the colonies at Dagenham and Canvey Island. But the ill-luck which was to dog Vermuyden's later ventures beset him almost at once. There was continuous and violent opposition to his plans from the local inhabitants, who disliked the alien invasion and mistrusted the objects of the adventurers.

In spite of local opposition which smouldered for fifteen years, much was achieved including the cutting of the dyke called the Dutch River, which took the waters of the Don directly into the Ouse, near Goole. Vermuyden was well supported by Charles I, who honoured him with a knighthood in 1629, and for some years the new settlers cultivated their lands in peace, building their own cottages and churches and peopling the lonely flats with windmills in the Dutch manner. But the shadows of civil dissension were lengthening and Vermuyden as a royal protegé and a foreigner, with all his schemes, was suspect. The opposition flared up one night in 1642, when the Parliamentarians at Lincoln received news that the Royalists were about to march into the Isle of Axholme from Yorkshire. Orders were given to break the dykes and pull up the sluice gates; the floods roared out over the land and in a few hours the work of years was undone.

In the meantime, Vermuyden had been in contact with the Earl of Bedford, trying to set on foot his plan for reclaiming the Cambridge Fens. In this he found himself in competition with another Dutchman, Westerdyke, who also submitted plans, but Vermuyden's superior organising ability and wider experience won the day. A formidable task faced him: the watery wastes from Boston to Ely were inhabited by the 'fen-slodgers' – a wild, strange people even more hostile to change than the inhabitants of Hatfield Chase. Vermuyden's workmen were attacked and their works pulled down: the streets and inns of Holbeach, Wisbech, Chatteris and Ely echoed to the ominous sounds of xenophobic balladry.

> The Dutchman hath a thirsty soul,
> Our cellars are subject to his call . . .
> To the new world in the moon away let us goe,
> For if the Dutch Colony get thither first,
> 'Tis a thousand to one but they'll drain that too.[18]

Vermuyden's schemes suffered disaster: under cover of the prevailing civil disorders his banks and dykes were broken down and by 1642 the greater part of the Fens again lay waste. It was not until 1649 after another triumph over his opponents (including once more his Dutch rival Westerdyke) that the work began again. By 1652 the works were declared to be complete, and at Ely Vermuyden read to the Lords Commissioners an address in which he claimed that in the North and Middle Levels, 40,000 acres of reclaimed land were already 'sown with coleseed, wheat and other winter grain besides innumerable quantities of sheep, cattle and other stock'. He concluded:

> I humbly desire that God may have the glory, for His blessing and bringing to perfection my poor endeavours, at the vast charge of the Earl of Bedford and his participants.[19]

Soon afterwards Vermuyden disappears from sight, a broken and disappointed man. But in spite of his failures, his achievements were considerable. A boggy wilderness was replaced by thousands of acres of the best land in Britain. Broad fields of corn waved where formerly only the wild fowl screamed and dived over the reeds and waters.

The Dutch not only showed the English how to reclaim their drowned acres from the sea; they also showed them how to plant, cultivate and graze them. It is almost impossible to be exact or categorical about innovations in agrarian history; we are drawn inevitably into a world of rural legend. Nevertheless, legend has its own importance and the number of times the Dutch appear in the shadowy annals of farming history in these years is significant, usually in connection with root crops or the scientific breeding of cattle. Antony Ashley, grandfather of the Earl of Shaftesbury, spent some time in the Netherlands and transcribed some of the works of the great cartographer Lucas Waghenaer (the author of the *Spieghel der Zeevaert*). He is also credited with the introduction of the cabbage into England from the Netherlands. But the rural England of Stuart times was in no mood to abandon its conservative agrarian traditions for the methodical and scientific ways of the Dutch. Too many country squires were away at the wars, too many estates devastated by sword and fire or ruined by debt. Another hundred years elapsed before English farming was ready to adopt the more rational methods by which the Dutch had already raised productivity far beyond that in other countries. The chief one was the process whereby clover and turnips were embodied into the crop-rotation. This not only made for a more efficient and economical method of combined arable and stock farming but also prepared the way for the later achievements of Bakewell and Curwen in developing new and improved strains of cattle and sheep.

Both crops had been in systematic use in the Netherlands for many years, and it seems more than likely that Lord Townshend ('Turnip' Townshend as he became known) who had been ambassador to the United Provinces and who is usually given the credit for their introduction into England on a large scale, had noted in his painstaking way how successfully the Dutch used them. But Townshend on his great estate at Raynham in Norfolk probably only helped to generalise practices already known. Carrots had been imported as a crop into eastern England early in the seventeenth century from the Low Countries. Townshend's neighbours and rivals at Houghton, the Walpoles, had been growing turnips as stock feed on the Dutch plan many years earlier. Great quantities of clover-seed were imported in these years from Amsterdam by west country merchants. The seed was usually unloaded from the Dutch ships on to the quays at Topsham about April to be sold at Exeter or Tiverton markets in time for the sowing season. There it was bought by the travelling chapmen who distributed to their customers all over Devon, Somerset, Dorset and Wiltshire.

According to Vermuyden's opponents, the crops which the Dutch engineers planned to grow on their reclaimed land – cole-seed and rape seed – also came from the Netherlands; they were 'but Dutch commodities and but trash and trumpery'. But the Dutch knew better: the crops they sowed were designed to remove excess salt from the soil reclaimed from the sea.

At the same time the famous breed of Frisian cattle was making its appearance in Britain. Mortimer, writing in 1707, remarked that 'the long-legged short-horned Cow of the Dutch breed' found in Lincolnshire and Kent was the best breed for milking.[20] By the end of the eighteenth century great strides had been made and the famous Lincolnshire red short-horn emerged as the final triumphant combination of the Dutch and northern English strains.

Nor must we overlook the more exotic exports from Holland. Many an English merchant from London or the west country, visiting his Amsterdam correspondent to look over samples of linens from Germany or silks from Italy, would bring back a selection of bulbs for his garden, chosen for him perhaps by his Dutch friends from the *bollenvelden* at Haarlem or Bloemendaal. And tradition has it that it was Sir Matthew Decker, a wealthy Dutch merchant and financier settled at Richmond, who grew the first pineapple on English soil. Next after the Dutch, the English were the first to rationalise and reform their agriculture. They did so with the help of Dutch methods, Dutch engineers, Dutch capital investment. Thus they greatly improved farming productivity, achieving a large measure of national sufficiency in food. Other neighbours of the Dutch benefited too – northern France, Denmark, southern Sweden, north-western Germany all bore the marks of Dutch agricultural methods. The rest of Europe was much slower to follow. But after the French Revolution began the process of breaking the hold of feudal custom throughout Europe, the combination of Dutch and English cropping methods was increasingly seen wherever mixed farming was possible.

Dutch, Flemish, and Walloon immigrants also played a vital role in creating or stimulating new growth in manufacturing industry. As at Leyden and Abbeville, so at Norwich and Colchester, colonies of refugees, mainly from the Ypres region, rescued the decaying textile industries. Norwich 'stuffs' – light, bright, relatively cheap – and Colchester 'bays and says' rapidly acquired great popularity in home and export markets. In both towns the immigrants formed a substantial proportion of the population by 1600.

They had their own communal arrangements and laws, arranged by treaty with the citizens. They had the right to sell their own cloths and worship according to their own customs. There were other, smaller 'Dutch' colonies at Sandwich, Rye, Canterbury, Southampton, and of course London. Each centred on a church and all were plants of the same seed – the original colony at Sandwich, still in the age of the revolt against Spain a flourishing and conveniently placed port for refugees fleeing from Alva's persecutions. From Sandwich – the reception centre, as it were – weavers, carpenters, gardeners, printers, brewers, bakers, bookbinders, metal workers, and scores of other artisans had fanned out to west and north. The suburbs of Stuart London were full of Dutch craftsmen bringing new skills. One was Jan van Hamme who took out a patent in 1671 'for the art of makeinge tiles and porcelane and other earthenwares after the way practised in Holland'. Hence began the English Delft industry which spread later to Bristol and Liverpool.

Further north the colonies of Dutch engineers who drained the Fens had their churches at Sandtoft in north Lincolnshire and at Thorney. As far south as Cambridge they left their mark. At Fen Stanton cottages by the church still show their mounting gables. A mile across the meadows at Fen Drayton, gabled cottages said by local legend to have been built by Vermuyden stand by canals overgrown with weeds. By the church, carved in stone over a door, is the Dutch motto *Niet Zonder Arbijt* (Not Without Labour).

The strongest evidence of Anglo-Dutch trade comes from these eastern areas. Henry Bell's Custom House at King's Lynn might well masquerade as the *Waaghuis* in Gouda or Alkmaar. Many East Anglian houses were built of bricks and tiles shipped from

Rotterdam or Flushing as cargoes or ballast. The Old Meeting House at Norwich had a pavement of Dutch bricks and tiles brought back by Walloon refugees who returned from exile in Holland. Until recently Dutch tiles were still abundant in East Anglia. But all round the English coast an observant visitor can usually spot the evidence of Dutch trade or immigration.

Gradually the Dutch colonies of East Anglia, London and Devon lost their identity and became merged with their English neighbours. These colonies were the product of the positive, expansive age of the Dutch. Sometimes they were evidence of the deliberate policy of governments of attracting to England people with skills as yet unfamiliar to England. Was too much English cloth being exported undyed? Skilled dyers must be attracted from Holland by privileges of easy nationality. Did the new 'sugar house' at Glasgow need a skilled sugar boiler? An Amsterdammer took the job. The highly progressive shipbuilding industry of Zaandam not only produced a rational design for the flyboat: it manufactured the new model by rational methods that included standardised and easily replaceable components. Hundreds of Dutch-built flyboats were in English service until the last quarter of the seventeenth century. The same industry may have suggested another technique. A German visitor to Bristol in the early nineteenth century observed:

The number of small wooden houses of the sixteenth century . . . detract much from its appearance. These are called the Dutch houses, having been imported ready made and having formed at one time an important article of traffic between this country and Holland. What would the Englishman of the present day say of the idea of importing a dwelling house from the Continent?

6 The age of observation: science

Scholars have often been tempted to exaggerate the influence of scientists and scientific method on economic development in the past. It seems certain that manufacturing *industry* progressed by the accumulation of technological gadgets, small advances by practical men, rather than through the conscious application of scientific principles. But there were reasons why the expansion of the Dutch economy should owe an uncommon debt to pure and applied science. For its basis was seaborne trade, shipping and navigation. And it was at this point that science could most effectively make an impact on economic growth by making long voyages at sea safer, quicker and less costly. In so far as this meant designing more efficient ships (the *fluit* has been described elsewhere) the work was largely the empirical innovations of sailors and shipbuilders. But to improve navigation called together the talents of mathematicians, engravers, printers, cartographers, instrument makers, lens grinders and others.

A key figure in this unique partnership between science and technology was Simon Stevin, tutor to Prince Maurice, son of William the Silent, Stevin was another instance of the Dutch Republic's debt to its less fortunate southern neighbour. He was born at Bruges but moved to Leyden where the Prince inaugurated a chair of mathematics and engineering for him at the new university, founded to celebrate the defeat of the besieging Spaniards in 1572. Stevin was the brain of that academy of military studies which Maurice made the most famous in Europe. Stevin tells a significant anecdote of the Prince. When His Excellency wanted to master the secrets of perspective, he first of all sent for the most celebrated painting masters he could find. But he was dissatisfied with the casual and unscientific way they shortened lines and altered angles by guesswork. The Prince wanted to proceed by ascertaining causes and finding mathematical proof for them.

Stevin (his motto was *Miracle is No Miracle*) pioneered in a number of fields of science – the decimal system, ballistics, fortification, as well as pure mathematics. He contributed to the progress of navigation with his book, *De Havenvinding*, which was charmingly translated into English and French immediately as *The Haven-Finding Art* and *Le Trouve-Port*. The English translator was Edward Wright, a fellow of Gonville and Caius College, Cambridge, a name still known to sailors, for it was he who in 1599 introduced the 'time chart' in the same form used today – a notable advance towards reliable mathematical navigation. Wright observed in his dedication (to Prince Henry, James I's eldest son who died in adolescence) that Prince Maurice had ordered all Dutch ship-masters to use Stevin's method and navigational tables and to report to the admiralty their observations of the deviations of the compass needle. Desiring to encourage others to follow suit, the Stadholder had caused translations to be made in French and Latin. Wright, in turn, by making an English translation available, wished to be 'a furtherer of so good a purpose of so famous a personage'.

Men like Stevin and Wright were beginning to ask not what *purpose* but what *process* lay behind the phenomena of nature. Qualitative theory, in which anything, miracles included, could be comprehended, was giving way to quantitative theory and analysis. One reason for this was that man was discovering tools and instruments by which short-range practical problems could be tackled. The phrase *sub specie aeternitatis*, which no one could translate but everyone could understand, was coined by Spinoza at a time when the very possibility of more immediate apprehension made men understand how abstract and imprecise was the old Aristotelianism that dealt in 'essence', 'matter', 'form', and the like. This discovery of mathematics and mathematical instruments as a tool for the solution not only of immediate problems of natural science but of social science (like demography, social welfare,

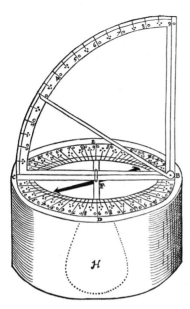

national income, balance of trade calculations and the like) was one of the most important advances of the seventeenth century. The consciousness that a new era had dawned comes in the dedication of another work of Edward Wright's on *Errors in Navigation* when he writes that:

> even God himselfe apparently seemeth to aime at this marke; for else what shoulde it meane that within these few score yeeres Hee hath discovered to the world the greatest and rarest secrets, farre exceeding all that could be found out by the art and industries of man in divers thousands of yeeres before . . .[21]

Mankind was launched into the Age of Observation. In the same year (1608) there appeared the earliest history of the Low Countries in English, the translation of the first infantry manual, the first illustrated book of instructions for English flower painting, the first petitions to the States General for a monopoly of the manu-

The most direct influence of Simon Stevin (1548–1620),
the great mathematician of Leyden, was through his pupil
Prince Maurice of Nassau, to whom he taught ballistics and
many forms of military engineering which revolutionised warfare.
(*Left*) A figure from his *Haven-Finding*.

facture and sale of optical instruments. Nowhere was the business
of scientific observation more energetically pursued than in
Holland. The principal tool of this phase of science, whether it was
directed to the investigation of the external world of the heavens
or the internal world of protozoä and spermatozoä, was the lens.
It did for the human eye what the steam engine was later to do for
muscle, what the computer was to do for the human brain. Almost
every scientist of the Age of Observation in Holland was also a
craftsman who knew how to grind his own lenses.

Like the painters, the scientists were also craftsmen. Their
central task was the anatomy of the universe. For the Dutch, as for
the English and Italians, this was a century fascinated by the
imagery of 'anatomy' – *The Anatomy of Wit*, *The Anatomy of the
World*, *The Anatomy of Melancholy*. Second only after Padua,
Leyden University became the leading centre of its study. Van
Wesel and Pieter Paauw became the pioneers of the new anatomy.
Annually the Guild of Physicians and Surgeons anatomised
publicly the body of a criminal executed in the city. The engraving
(1610) of Paauw's *Theatrum Anatomicum* is the earliest pictorial
record of a theatre in Holland.

Leyden owned two other scientific laboratories. In 1632 the
Curators built an *Observatorium Astronomicum* on the roof of the
university to house the unique quadrant constructed for Snellius,
the professor of mathematics who had discovered the law of
refraction and could claim to be the father of triangulation. This
was the method by which he measured the distance and bearing
between Alkmaar and Bergen-op-Zoom in 1617. By solving the
triangle he found the meridian distance between the two towns,
measuring their latitudes by the Pole Star. A little way away was the
famous *Hortus Botanicus*, much praised and imitated in England
and the nursery of tulips of great beauty and rarity. These were to
give rise to that curious exhibition of hysteria, the Dutch tulipo-

Development of anatomical studies stood out in the Dutch scientific movement. Rembrandt was fascinated by anatomy as one aspect of the truth about the human body; also, as in the case of *The Anatomy Lesson of Professor Tulp*, because it allowed him to lend a macabre intensity to a group portrait. Tulp's audience is the surgeons' guild and the corpse that of a criminal. Public anatomising was an annual event.

mania later in the century, when wild speculation took place in the price of rare tulip bulbs.

In Holland more than anywhere else, pure science merged imperceptibly into applied, theory into technology. Neither Stevin, Snellius, nor Huygens despised the challenge of those practical problems that stood in the way of safer navigation and longer voyages. Perhaps here again, as with the vivid flowering of the arts, the explanation of this intense blend of pure and applied science may lie partly in the simple conditions of life and society in Holland – a relatively dense population gathered into sizeable towns; and facing the challenge of earning the best living they could with little or nothing in the way of natural resources. To promote their unique exchange economy and exploit its potentialities to the maximum, education was a necessity, not an ornament. From the age of three onwards, Dutch children were inserted into an educational machine, passing through primary school to Latin school, thence to university or an 'Illustrious School'. Literacy was in consequence more widely spread than elsewhere in Europe. Special attention was paid to handwriting which often achieved standards of high elegance. Hence those widespread talents of engraving that helped to create a school of cartography and hydrography. Thus in one way and another Dutch society saw to it that its members were equipped for the world they had to make their living in. Here, as in Scotland, respect for education sprang from the knowledge that without it everyone would be the poorer.

This is not to say that the scientific achievements of seventeenth-century Holland can be explained simply in terms of a response to material or economic need. Science and technology, as has been stressed, were closely allied with mathematics, and mathematics with philosophy. At every point, the observer can watch disinterested scientific curiosity and the quest for pure knowledge coming into play. Botany, biology, microscopy, optics, statistics, measurement

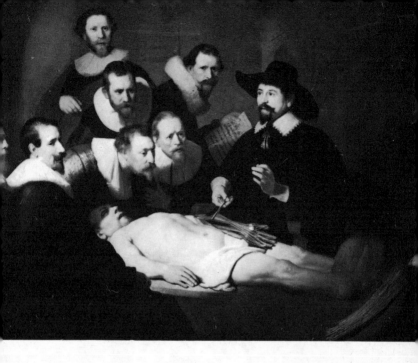

for architectural design, anatomy, astronomy – all were evidence that a simple materialist interpretation of the Age of Observation in Holland is inadequate to explain much that was finest and most influential in Dutch scientific thought. It was these achievements of pure science which were most regarded outside the boundaries of Holland and throughout later ages.

In one respect the sciences in Holland resembled the arts. When their roots were not indigenous they were Italian. In so far as they had recognisable and direct progeny they were English. Yere as so often the Dutch were performing, indirectly, their characteristic broking function, absorbing, modifying and extending the experience of the ancient cultures of the Mediterranean and transmitting them northwards and westwards across the English Channel. Dutch relations with the Royal Society of England illustrate the process very clearly.

The Royal Society was founded while England was still in the

The science of anatomy, widely pursued, was
a particular study at Amsterdam and Leyden.
In the famous circular anatomy theatre at Leyden,
humour mingles with medical learning.

99

first fine frenzy of post-Cromwellian royalism, on the crest of a wave of optimistic humanism which made the political and theo-logical controversies of six decades seem stale, arid and unprofitable. One of its main aims from its foundation in 1661 was to bring English philosophers, inventors, and experimenters back into touch with their contemporaries on the continent. Correspondence with continental philosophers formed the first *Philosophical Transactions* of the Society. No doubt the appointment of the first secretary, Henry Oldenburg, a Bremener, was made partly with the object of furthering such correspondence. From the start the Royal Society was universal in its outlook, its membership cosmopolitan.

We know from Evelyn, Pepys, and other writers that there were at this time in England a number of Dutchmen of energy and initiative who brought with them to England that inventiveness and resource for which the Dutch were famous throughout the world. Besides the engineers like Vermuyden, Westerdyke and Croppen-burgh, there was the ingenious Kiviet, who had projects for wharfing the Thames with bricks, for draining the meres round Newmarket and growing cole-seed instead, and for popularising a fuel called 'loullies', a kind of coal briquette, manufactured at Maastricht.

An even more intriguing figure is Cornelius Drebbel, a native of Alkmaar, who came to England in 1604 possibly with Constantijn Huygens. Drebbel was a strange character, half alchemist, half scientist, typical of the early Jacobean age of Donne and the metaphysical poets, an age which could hold both Sir Thomas Browne and Bacon. Drebbel commended himself to King James (who had a notoriously soft spot for sorcerers) and was granted an annuity and quarters at Eltham Palace. He rapidly acquired a reputation for 'great sagacity as an inventor of machines'. Many of his alleged inventions belong evidently to the alchemical side of his genius, but they are worth mentioning as showing the pseudoscientific interests of contemporary society, and the background of magicians' art from which the scientific revival of the Restoration emerged. He is among the many claimants of his time to be the inventor of a machine for producing perpetual motion. He claimed to have invented a submarine boat which could be navigated from Westminster to Greenwich; to have made machines to produce rain, hail and lightning, as well as a device for producing wintry temperatures 'of which he made an experiment, as it is pretended, in Westminster Hall at the instance of the King of England: and that the cold was so great as to be unsupportable'. No doubt his ingenuity came in useful in staging those fantastically elaborate masques of which James I was so fond.

Drebbel has claims to be taken more seriously. He turned his attention to devising weapons for naval warfare and was apparently in charge of the fire ships of the expedition to La Rochelle. His masterpiece was the discovery of a method of dyeing wool scarlet by means of cochineal and tin solutions; his method was quickly applied at the textile dye works in Bow. At Leyden his process was used by his son-in-law, variously known as Kuffler, Cuffler or Keffler. They were linked with the Royal Society by their publication in 1662 of an account entitled *An Apparatus to the History of the Common Practices of Dyeing*, which incorporates the work of Drebbel, his son Jacob, and his son-in-law. Needless to say, Drebbel also appears among the early projectors connected with the fen drainage schemes.

These were offshoots of contemporary scientific and technological developments in Holland where, in spite of the dogmatic opposition of the predestinarian Calvinists, a vigorous school of science had grown up since the beginning of the seventeenth century. Among the early members and fellows of the Royal Society there are some distinguished Dutch names. Three of the greatest Dutch scientists – Christiaan Huygens, Antony van Leeuwenhoek

CASTEEL VAN NAMEN EN COEHORN HET
DUYVELS HUYS ETC.VEROVERT BOUFLERS WEG GEVOERT

Tangena Exc.

and Hermannus Boerhaave, accepted fellowship of the Society. All were men of wide scientific interests and broad vision. The activities of each covered what nowadays would be regarded as a number of different fields of scientific investigation. Huygens we now remember primarily as a physicist, but he was also a mathematician, an astronomer and a mechanical scientist. Leeuwenhoek, a draper of Delft, is famous chiefly as a microscopist, but he was also an anatomist and an entomologist. Boerhaave's name was famous throughout the world of medicine, but he was almost as distinguished as a chemist, as a botanist, and as a mathematician. If they were not narrow or specialist in their scientific work, neither were they parochial in their general outlook. They were good Europeans.

Most of Huygens's important discoveries were communicated to the world through the agency of the *Philosophical Transactions* of the Royal Society. Leeuwenhoek made known many of his most striking discoveries to the Royal Society by means of well over a hundred papers communicated to them as well as more than twenty papers communicated to the Paris Academy of Sciences. Huygens and Leeuwenhoek both symbolise the typical contemporary relationship between applied and pure science. Like a number of the early Dutch scientists they both graduated from the school of practical craftsmanship in optical glass technique which had grown up in seventeenth-century Holland. This remarkable industry was the nursery of early Dutch science.

The art of grinding and polishing lenses for telescopes was specially important to a community like the Dutch, whose wealth depended on seaborne trade and whose very existence hung on the grain ships which brought the Netherlanders' food from northern Europe. An elementary knowledge of astronomy was vital to the Dutch seamen and navigators; whatever their scientists could provide in the way of telescopes, binoculars, spectacles and navigational instruments was welcome to merchants and government alike. From that need came the scientists, evolving gradually from craftsmen, grinding and polishing lenses for spectacles and telescopes, into applied scientists working to solve practical problems of navigation, and from applied science moving steadily into the wider spheres of pure science. The most important point in this process was the invention of the telescope in Holland in the early seventeenth century.

The discovery itself was for long in dispute. The three claimants were Lippershey and Jansen, the spectacle makers of Middelburg, and Metius, the mathematician of Alkmaar. Examination of the manuscripts in the Huygens collection at Leyden University has put it beyond dispute that the real inventor was Lippershey, who was given 900 florins by a committee of the States General, together with a commission to execute two more telescopes of similar design. (Here, as always, the Dutch authorities showed a remarkably modern appreciation of the value of scientific application to the problems of commerce and navigation.)

These early Dutch telescopes all consisted of one convex and one concave lens (of the type commonly known as Galilean), and were rapidly found in use in England, as well as in France, Italy and Germany. A few years earlier, Johann and Zacharias Jansen had built the first compound microscope, combining a strong biconcave and strong biconvex lens. Here, then, is one nursery of physical and biological science in seventeenth-century Holland. From this nursery came Huygens, who never forgot the art of polishing a lens – an accomplishment which led directly to his great astronomical and physical discoveries; Leeuwenhoek, who first ground and polished a lens of such short focus as to make possible a simple microscope better than the contemporary compound microscope; Spinoza made his living as a lens-grinder; lastly Boerhaave himself was still close enough to this technical, practical side of science to translate Huygens's treatise on glass-polishing into Latin.

Christiaan Huygens was born at the Hague in 1629, the son of Constantijn Huygens, Secretary to three Princes of Orange and Lord of Zuylichem. Christiaan began his remarkable career at the age of thirteen, when he was already a considerable mathematician and an expert on practical mechanics. His first experiments attracted the attention of Descartes who wrote of him that 'he will excel in this science, in which I can scarcely see anyone who knows anything of it.' Most of his early work was practical. In 1658 he published his *Brief Demonstration of the Use of the Chronometer for ascertaining Longitude* and demonstrated a model of the newly invented pendulum clock. In 1659 he was at work on a telescope with which he hoped to explain the surprising appearances of Saturn. It was in the course of these observations that he discovered one of Saturn's satellites (Titan) and the

TAB. XXX.

existence of Saturn's rings. The following year he communicated
to the Royal Society a paper on the art of polishing lenses for
telescopes. He had already used a telescope of twelve-feet focal
length, while in his *Systema Saturnium* he described his invention
of the micrometer, an instrument which could be used for measuring
small angular distances with a telescope or for finding the dimen-
sions of small objects with a microscope. This Huygens used to
determine the diameters of planets. By 1681 he was using lenses of

The lens was the principal instrument by which the new scientific observations of the seventeenth century were advanced. Many Dutch scientists of the time made their own lenses: (*right*) Christiaan Huygens (1629–95), and (*left*) an aerial telescope which he built.

great focal length to overcome the poor definition characteristic of this type of telescope; these were mounted on high poles and connected to the eye-piece by means of rods and cords. Three of these object glasses of 123, 180, and 210 feet focal length, are still in the possession of the Royal Society.

Meanwhile Colbert had succeeded in attracting him to France. From 1666 to 1681, Huygens worked in the seclusion of the Bibliothèque du Roi and from thence dedicated a number of works to his royal patron. Colbert no doubt hoped he had captured a major technologist. He was not far wrong.

Huygens was experimenting on the newly-invented air-pump into which he introduced a number of improvements; here again was the beginning of an invention which was later to revolutionise the mining industry and ultimately all industrial organisation. The most important inventions for which he was solely responsible were the micrometer and the pendulum chronometer. Meanwhile, he had evolved a number of scientific principles which rank him with Newton – the laws governing the collision of elastic bodies, the wave theory of light (known as the 'Principle of Huygens') and the theory of polarisation of light. According to one biographer he was

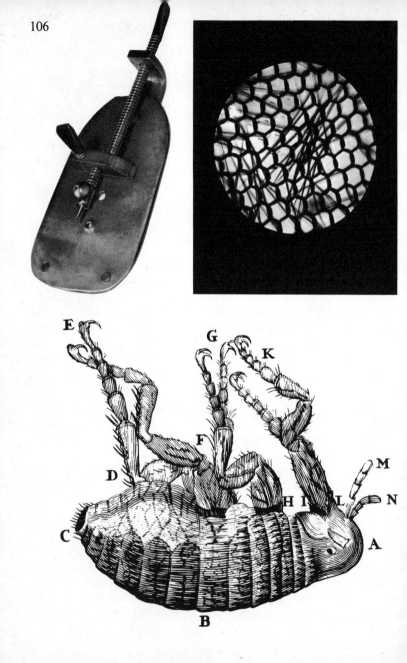

(*left*) The microscope of Anthonie van Leeuwenhoek (1632–1723), the Dutch pioneer of modern microscopy. (*right*) The eye of a fly, recently photographed through the original microscope. (*below*) A minutely accurate insect drawing from Leeuwenhoek's *Little Animals*.

an amiable, cheerful, worthy man: and in all respects as good as he was great. Huygens loved a quiet and studious life, and perhaps through fear of interruption never married.[22]

The basis of Leeuwenhoek's work, like Huygens's, was the perspective instrument, but while Huygens had moved into astronomy, Leeuwenhoek devoted himself to the study of the structure of small bodies with the aid of the microscope. He was introduced to the Royal Society by another great Dutch scientist, Regnier de Graaf, the physiologist, in 1673, and became a Fellow of the Society in 1680. His discoveries were mostly communicated to the world throughout the *Philosophical Transactions*. His list of achievements is remarkable. In 1668 he confirmed Malphighi's demonstration of the blood capillaries and in 1674 gave the first accurate description of the red blood corpuscles, which he found to be circular in man but oval in frogs and fishes. Three years later he described and illustrated the spermatozoä of animals and investigated the structure of teeth, the crystalline lens, a human muscle, and living and decaying plant organisms. His account of the flea from its first emergence from the egg was his masterpiece. Other enquiries were into the blighting of trees by aphides and into the generation of eels (which contemporary learned men supposed to be produced from the dew without any ordinary processes of generation).

In a superstitious and inaccurate age, when even the scientific ideas of the expert were often mingled with a good deal of mystical mumbo-jumbo, Leeuwenhoek's work is a model of conscientious and accurate scientific research. Leeuwenhoek is buried in the Oude Kerk at Delft, alongside Tromp and Piet Hein. 'As everyone, O Wanderer,' his epitaph concludes 'has respect for old age and wonderful parts, tread this spot with reverence; here lies grey Science buried with Leeuwenhoek'.

Hermannus Boerhaave (1668–1738) was elected FRS in 1729,

towards the end of a life devoted to medical research and teaching. Boerhaave's election was *honoris causa*. His greatest work was done: in the Netherlands and throughout Europe he was already 'the great Boerhaave'. Already the story was told of the letter merely addressed 'Boerhaave – Europe' which reached its destination safely. Boerhaave was born at Voorhout, a small village about two miles from Leyden. His father intended him to go into the Church, and his first studies at Leyden University were in divinity. But gradually the compass of his reading and activities grew: in addition to theology, he read philosophy, mathematics, botany, anatomy and chemistry. For a long time medicine was a hobby with him until gradually his genius became apparent. In 1709 he became Professor of Medicine and Botany, and ten years later, Professor of Chemistry. In these posts, his impressive abilities as a lecturer were devoted to stressing the essential simplicity of true medicine, exploding the fallacies of the alchemists and metaphysical writers and replacing his science on a sound basis of observation and experiment.

His published works constitute a vast library of research in medicine, botany and chemistry. With Huygens he is linked by his translation of his papers on the art of lens-making; with Leeuwenhoek by his application of Leeuwenhoek's methods to physiological research. His main service to medicine was to reduce it from superstitious theory to respectable practice, to bring it down from the bookshelves to the bedside. As Samuel Johnson wrote in his obituary of Boerhaave in 1738, Boerhaave was not a theorist:

in his examinations of the sick he was remarkably circumstantial and particular. He well knew the originals of Distempers are often at a distance from their visible Effects, that to conjecture where Certainty may be obtained, is either vanity or Negligence, and that Life is not to be sacrificed, either to an Affectation of quick Discernment or of crowded Practice but may be required if trifled away, at the hand of the Physician.[23]

Undoubtedly, Johnson was gratified that in an age when science was already beginning to be identified with atheism or at any rate scepticism, here was a great scientist who seemed to know where to draw the line between science and religion. Here are the last paragraphs of Johnson:

Thus died Boerhaave, a Man formed by Nature for great Designs, and guided by Religion in the Exertion of his abilities. He was of a robust and athletic Constitution of Body, so harden'd by early Severities, and wholesome Fatigue, that he was insensible of any Sharpness of Air or Inclemency of Weather . . .

He knew the importance of his own Writings to Mankind, and lest he might, by a Roughness and Barbarity of Stile, too frequent among men of Great Learning, disappoint his own Intentions, and make his Labours less useful, he did not neglect the politer Arts of Eloquence and Poetry. Thus was his learning at once various and exact, profound and agreeable . . .

So far was this Man from being made Impious by Philosophy, or vain by knowledge, or by Virtue, that he ascribed all his Abilities to the Bounty, and all his Goodness to the Grace of God. May his Example extend its influences to his Admirers and Followers! May Those who study his writings imitate his life, and those who endeavour after his Knowledge aspire likewise to his Piety.

Boerhaave had admirers and followers in many European countries. Both as physician and physiologist he was an inspiring teacher who knew all his pupils individually and maintained a lively and continuous correspondence with many of them. Scottish students, and Dissenters from the north of England especially, flocked to Leyden to study medicine in the wake of their predecessors who had studied law and theology. The majority of the original founders and teachers of the Edinburgh Medical School were pupils of Boerhaave; John Fothergill (1712–80) of a Wensleydale Quaker family who became the leader of the new London school of practical medicine was another. In return Boerhaave always generously acknowledged his debt to contemporary English scientists, especially to Newton and to Sydenham, whom he always called 'the British Hippocrates'. It is difficult to overrate the influence of Boerhaave, standing as he does at the beginning of a century which saw such great strides in social medicine and in consequence the beginning of that growth of population which in Britain is linked with an agricultural and industrial revolution destined to transform society.

Finally, no activity was more essential or characteristic of this maritime society than the combination of art, craft and science called cartography. The first necessity for the merchant venturing into overseas trade is a ship. For a little time – while he is content to navigate local waters with the help of local knowledge of tides, currents and coasts – he may need little more. But it will not be long before he is emboldened to go further afield: then he will call in the aid of the geographers and cartographers to supply him with aids to navigation.

The history of cartography in the sixteenth and seventeenth centuries is closely associated with a number of contemporary events – the geographical discoveries of the Portuguese, Dutch and British, the growth of sea borne trade – especially Dutch trade –

the scientific enquiries set on foot by the requirements of the navigators, and the development of printing and engraving, which reached a high degree of excellence in both the southern and northern Netherlands. No other people could rival the Dutch in their achievements in all these fields; practically all the maps published in the sixteenth and the first half of the seventeenth century can be attributed to the school of cartographers which first grew up in Holland in the sixteenth century.

The first two great map-makers of this period were both Flemings – Gerard Kremer (better known as Mercator) 1512–94, and his friend Abraham Ortelius (1527–98). Their greatest work dates from the time before Spanish dynastic and religious ambitions had divided the Low Countries: historically and economically, their work is a legacy of the great days of Antwerp as the main entrepôt of western Europe. Mercator and Ortelius were an ideal combination of academic and practical ability: Mercator was a mathematician by training; Ortelius a merchant who was attracted by his friend's work to the scientific study of geography. Together, they helped to free geography from the tyranny of Ptolemy and the fantastic traditions of medieval legend and inaccuracy.

Mercator's greatest work was his map of the world, as then known, on the projection principle, with parallels and meridians at right angles; Ortelius's the *Theatrum Orbis Terrarum*. Already the custom of having English maps engraved in Holland was beginning; Mercator engraved Camden's map of the British Isles in 1564. And the works of both were printed by Christopher Plantin and Van Ravelingen of Leyden. Already the way was paved for a school of scientific map-makers, collaborating with a school of engravers capable of work of the necessary clarity and precision. But so far cartography was still groping for general principles: it was the work of the next generation of cartographers of the Northern provinces to apply themselves to the solution of

The frontispiece to Waghenaer's
Mariner's Mirrour, translated into English
by Anthony Ashley in 1588. Known as
'Waggoners', these charts became part
of the standard equipment of European
navigators in the seventeenth century.

the problems of the navigators and to the production of – among other works – the county maps of England. Of the two, the makers of the hydrographic charts – especially Waghenaer and Blaeu – are the more important: it is impossible to overestimate their value to the seafaring community of western Europe in the seventeenth century.

Lucas Janszoon Waghenaer of Enkhuizen on the Zuiderzee, unlike Mercator, seems to have started his career as a pilot on a cargo ship trading from his native port. Coasting perilously round the shores of western Europe, he no doubt became only too conscious of the discrepancies and imperfections of the 'books of the ports' on which pilots then had to rely. These note-books merely gave the pilot the rough distance between one port of call and the next, the course he should try to steer, with possibly some scrappy information about the tides. In 1584, Waghenaer produced the first part of his *Spieghel der Zeevoert van de Navigatie der Westersche Zee*. This was a collection of charts of the coasts of Europe between the Zuiderzee and Cadiz, engraved on copper plates and printed at Leyden by Christopher Plantin. The following year, the second part followed, containing charts of the coasts of the North Sea and the Baltic. In 1592 came the *Thresoor der Zeevaert* covering the coasts of northern Ireland, Scotland and the Arctic. Finally in 1598, appeared the *Enchuyser Zeecaertboek*. Waghenaer's works represented an extraordinary advance in the nautical literature and cartography of Europe; while they were not free from error, they were relatively orderly and accurate and such mistakes as appeared were later corrected by his followers. Besides the charts, they contained an introduction on navigation, a kind of rough nautical almanac and sailing directions. Except for Mercator's engravings, Waghenaer's works contained the first examples in which charts were engraved on copper plates.

They met with immediate success, and nowhere were they more welcome than in England. The first Latin edition of Part I of the

Spieghel was dedicated to Queen Elizabeth, while the *Thresoor* contained summaries of the voyages of Drake and Cavendish. Lord Charles Howard of Effingham, lord admiral of England, quickly drew the attention of the Privy Council to the *Spieghel* as being an aid 'very necessary to our seamen,' and Anthony Ashley, Clerk to the Council, was instructed to translate it. The translation appeared at London in 1588 under the title *The Mariner's Mirrour* and became a standard work in England in the seventeenth and eighteenth centuries, so much so that it was responsible for a new term in hydrography – marine charts became known, by a debasing of the author's name, as 'waggoners'. Throughout the eighteenth century, we find 'Newest Waggoners' being advertised. In France, by an even stranger extension of the same process, they were known as 'chartiers.'

Waghenaer's charts were reprinted and improved in many respects by another great Dutch cartographer, William Janszoon Blaeu, in his *Licht der Zeevaert* which in 1617 was translated into English with the title *The Light of Navigation*. It would be no exaggeration to say that every seaman, British or Dutch, who sailed between Spitzbergen and the Canaries in the seventeenth and eighteenth centuries, used the charts of Waghenaer or one of his pupils.

Waghenaer's value was not overlooked by the Dutch authorities, who in their official encouragement of cartographers and inventors of navigational devices anticipated the British government by more than a century. In 1585 he was granted a pension by the States of Holland: further awards from the same authorities and from the States General followed in 1598. In the same year, he sat on a committee with Scaliger, the philologist, Stevin, Snellius and Van Collen (all mathematicians) to enquire into the claims of Plancius and Syvertzoon to have devised a process for working out longitude at sea – a problem which puzzled and to the end defeated the seventeenth century.

The first man definitely known to have made a marine time-keeper specifically designed to find longitude at sea was Christiaan Huygens. But Huygens's time-keeper was not provided with compensating mechanism, and the solution of the problem had to await the appearance of Harrison's chronometer almost a century later. Nevertheless, the incident shows how sailors, scientists and engravers collaborated with the authorities in seventeenth-century Holland to solve the problems of trade and navigation.

Close as was the connection of the Dutch hydrographers with England it was followed by even more intimate association in the persons of the two Hondiuses, the Jansens and the Blaeus, who mapped the English counties. The curious alliance of English and Dutch skill seems to have begun with two early Dutch engravers, Peter van der Keere and Jacob van Langeren, who engraved the maps of English counties by Christopher Saxton, John Speed and William Gamden, in the late sixteenth and early seventeenth centuries. The works of these three map-makers also formed the basis of the maps by later Dutch cartographers.

Blaeu's volumes were also reproduced many times later in the century. Henry Hondius, of Amsterdam, also produced a number of sectional maps of Great Britain including the first engraved map of the Great Level of the Fens in 1632. Whether Hondius had any special connection with the fen drainage schemes undertaken by the Dutch engineer Vermuyden, it is difficult to say. But his map is dedicated to the Duke of Bedford 'and the other adventurers'. It covers the area between Cambridge in the south, Peterborough in the west, Boston in the north and Brandon in the east. Ten years later, Vermuyden himself produced a map of exactly the same area (no doubt based on Hondius's) to illustrate his *Discourse touching the Drayning the Great Fennes* . . . Six years later, in 1648, John Blaeu followed with another map, no doubt carefully copied from the two previously described but distinguishable by having the title

GERARDUS MERCATOR NATUS
RUPELMUNDÆ II NON.MARTII ANNO
CIↃIↃXII VIXIT ANN.LXXXII M.VIII.D.
XXVI DENATUS V NON.DECEMBRIS
ANNO CIↃIↃXCIV.

IUDOCUS HONDIUS NATUS IN
PAGO FLANDRIÆ DICTO WACKENE XVI
KALEND NOVEMBRIS ANNO CIↃIↃLXIII
VIXIT ANN.XLVII.M.VII.D.XXIX DENAT
US XIV KAL MARTII ANNO CIↃIↃCXII.

set in the right-hand bottom corner in a rectangular panel, supported by an abundance of fruits, and agricultural implements. Some time before this Hondius and Blaeu had gone into partnership at Amsterdam: evidently they were already well-known in England, as John Evelyn made a point of visiting their shop during his visit to Holland in 1641, to buy maps and folios.

The great period of map-making in the northern Netherlands lasted a little more than a century: it was overtaken by the French school, founded about the middle of the seventeenth century by Sanson of Abbeville, who started by copying the works of the Dutch cartographers. Nevertheless, the tradition of the Amsterdam engravers lived on. English map-makers still went to Amsterdam

Mercator and Hondius, both of them Flemings, were among the founders of Netherlands cartography, essential to the expanding seaborne trade of the Republic. Jointly they represent one of the many debts owed by the new Republic to the Southern Netherlands, formally severed in 1609. The Hondius business continued in Amsterdam until late in the seventeenth century.

to have their maps engraved: we hear of Sir William Petty (who probably caught his enthusiasm for map-making while he was a student at Leyden) having his great map of Ireland 'engraved at Amsterdam for £1,000'.

The cartographers of the great period of the art in Holland took the whole world for their province: they mapped, with varying degrees of accuracy, not only the countries of Europe, but the continents of Africa, Asia and North and South America as well.

The hundreds of maps that issued from the presses of Amsterdam, Leyden and elsewhere substituted relatively systematic and scientific information for the legendary drawings and travellers' tales of earlier times. They circulated widely and still survive in large numbers as collectors' items. Few can have travelled further or survived more miraculously than one of Hondius's maps of England of 1590. A few years after it was published, two Dutch explorers, Heemskerck and Barentsz, tried to reach India by a north-west passage. They wintered in Nova Zembla and their adventures were published in several languages. More than two centuries later a *cache* of their equipment was recovered by a later expedition. It included a pair of compasses, a block-plane, nails, shoes and (*mirabile dictu*) fragments of the Hondius map. This exploit explains Fabian's remark to Sir Andrew Aguecheek in *Twelfth Night*.

You are now sailed to the North of my lady's opinion where you will hang like an icicle on a Dutchman's beard . . .[24]

7 The age of observation: visual and social arts

'Dutch painting in the seventeenth century' Professor G. J. Renier has written, 'was at the same time a cultural achievement and an unusually significant social phenomenon.' This dual character explains its impact both on the contemporary world and on subsequent ages. Few societies or periods have been so richly endowed with artists of genius as Holland in the early seventeenth century. Here we mean Holland in its proper sense: the province of Holland. Rembrandt, Van Mieris, Jan Steen, all came from Leyden, Cuyp came from Dordrecht, Van Goyen and Paul Potter from the Hague, De Hoogh and Vermeer from Delft, Ostade, Brouwer and Wouwermans from Haarlem. Amsterdam has been called a painters' colony. What an extraordinary flowering of talent in this small corner of the Netherlands, endowed by nature with no notable beauties of scenery except a changing expanse of sky interrupted by no intrusive mountains and relatively few trees!

The cultural achievement and the social phenomenon of Dutch painting were closely related. The Revolt and the military strategy and geographical facts by which the northern provinces were enabled to emerge independent and victorious had a profound influence also on Netherlands art. Devotional art such as had flourished especially in the southern Netherlands, associated with religious movements like the Brethren of the Common life, or even the mystical scenes of Hieronymus Bosch, came to an end. When religion came back into Dutch painting it was in the great dramatic tableaux of Rembrandt, many from the Old Testament. The genre was dramatic and humanist rather than devotional. Instead, portraiture, still life, landscape, interiors and 'social' scenes now became the most popular forms. Previously they had been adjuncts to, or elements in, biblical or devotional pictures. Now they acquired an autonomous value of their own.

As the new Protestant society of the north emerged, the nobility dwindled in numbers and wealth. The Church and court as institutions of patronage disappeared. Princes of Orange lived in what might be called 'palaces' but which were in reality large houses appropriate to patricians rather than to royalty. De Witt, the Grand Pensionary of Holland, lived simply and modestly, usually walking on foot rather than riding by carriage, eschewing any form of display and cultivating no entourage. The old court culture disappeared in the north. In the Spanish Netherlands it survived, and with it counter-Reformation Baroque that reached its greatest glories with Peter Paul Rubens. Rubens points the contrast. He himself lived like a prince. Compared with his penurious Dutch contemporaries he enjoyed a princely income.

Now naturalism began to replace the grandeur, heroism, sensualism and mysticism that characterised both the earlier Netherlands art and the art of the Baroque. Strong elements of naturalism had been present in much earlier Netherlands art. Late medieval portraits, crowd scenes and landscapes can all be found embodying brilliant touches of photographic realism. But now, along with the isolating of the secular subject matter came a new concentration on observation and representation. Here and there artists like Jan Both and Nicolas Berchem continued to work for patrons who wanted landscape in the Italian tradition; but it was a dwindling genre. The future – the two middle quarters of the century – lay with the naturalists – with De Hooch and Vermeer for those with a taste for domestic scenes, with Nicolas Maes or Jan Steen for those who liked sentiment or social realism. Arnold Hauser has summed up the characteristics of this phase as follows: 'The new middle class naturalism is a style not only to make spiritual things visible, but all visible things a spiritual experience'.[25]

It was the triumph of the Holland painters that they succeeded in depicting the ordinary things of everyday life with a passionate intensity that has never been surpassed. Holland became the home of the miraculous realism that illuminated the caterpillar crawling on the flower, the iridescence of a lobster shell, the refraction of a wineglass, the light falling on an apple or a distant grove or tree's, the wrinkles on an old woman's face. Samuel Pepys was fascinated by the *trompe l'oeil* of a drop of water on a flower by Verelst: 'it is worth going twenty miles to see it'. He went back time and again to the house of Mr Povey to see that 'piece of perspective' behind the door of a closet: 'then I saw there is nothing but only a plain picture hung upon a wall'.

Middle class? In a sense, yes. Undoubtedly, the tastes, beliefs, and economic circumstances of their patrons set certain limits to the painter's scope and choice of subject matter as well as its treatment. Rich merchants, shopkeepers, even peasants, bought pictures not as conscious patrons of the arts, but to add to the furnishing and decoration of their houses. A painting was simply another piece of furniture (there are still worse ways of setting about art appreciation). The painter was a supplier of goods like any other craftsman, though, as has sometimes been suggested, paintings may have flourished more abundantly because outlets for the investment of surplus were scarce in a small country. Pride, ostentation, snobbery, all played their immodest part in the game. Molenaer could paint a picture of a shipowner surrounded by his family and pointing proudly to the ninety-two ships he owned. Yet in other paintings, very rich men are depicted in the modest dress and austere surroundings becoming to a Calvinist.

The pictures in a Dutch home of any class were part of the invested wealth that the home represented. Significantly, the word for 'beautiful' in Dutch (*schoon*) came to mean 'clean'. The original meaning was virtually abandoned. The unbelievable cleanliness and tidiness of the Dutch scene was connected with this same phenomenon. The town, like the house, represented an intensive investment of capital. Space was too precious to be squandered. Yet the Dutch also bought paintings because they enjoyed them. Their pride was

A backyard scene by Pieter de Hooch, master of the domestic genre. Probably painted before he moved from Delft to Amsterdam and became more fashionable, it portrays a household of moderately wealthy position. National Gallery, London.

The first act of the Calvinist reformers was to remove all the images, pictures and ritual decoration from churches in the Protestantised regions. Nevertheless, Dutch artists (in particular Saanredam, the hunchback of Haarlem) succeeded in creating a special genre of these vast buildings and in making a virtue of this stark unadorned quality as in St Bavo's Church, Haarlem. The picture was a parting gift by the States General to Charles II on his Restoration in 1660.

expressed in the habit of naming streets after painters. (The English, with a great literary culture, have no Shakespeare or Shelley Streets. Roads and squares in England are named after great military victories or titled ground landlords, and in France after politicians and generals.)

Historians nowadays are much concerned with the explanation of social phenomena. Yet nothing eludes explanation so frustratingly as these explosions of collective and individual genius that have produced the world's greatest art and literature. The key to the Dutch golden age, as of others, may lie partly in a better understanding of the patronage which society provided for the artists. There is, alas, no enquiry into patronage in Holland comparable to Francis Haskell's study of the patrons of the Italian Renaissance.[21] Enough evidence is available, however, to show that patronage was widespread – but thinly spread. The Republic inherited a situation from earlier times, before the Revolt, when there were as many painters in Antwerp as butchers and bakers. Many of the great Dutch masters had to endure grinding poverty. Frans Hals, Hobbema and Ruysdael all ended their days in the almshouse. Hercules Seghers took to drink. Van Laar committed suicide. Vermeer was constantly tormented by creditors and died heavily in debt to his baker. Often clients lent money, on tough terms, to the penurious artist who then had to work his passage back to solvency. Rembrandt at one time owed a great patron forty thousand florins. Debts of this sort, mainly to rich Amsterdam clients, doubtless help to explain his feverish pace and output which probably hastened his end. More practical colleagues eked out a living by doing other things. Van Goyen traded in tulips, Van de Velde in linen, Jan Steen was an innkeeper. Others dealt in pictures.

The painter's life was hard and often short. Like other craftsmen – they were mainly working men – the artists had their gild. They learnt their trade like other tradesmen. There was little theorising or speculating on the deeper implications of their calling. The apprentice cleaned the master's brushes and swept the studio; as a journeyman he would be allowed to sketch backgrounds and small figures in the master's canvases. Yet when he became a fully-fledged gild member the monetary rewards were still meagre. What kept the profession going was the steady persistence of demand, rather than any expectation of high rewards.

The golden age lasted little more than half a century. By the third quarter the greatest names had gone. The last quarter of the century already marked the beginning of a decline which gathered pace in the early years of the next century. What continues to astonish generation after generation about the Dutch achievement is how a school based on purely technical training, and subject to limitations imposed by patrons whose own ideas of art were often narrow and simple, triumphantly broke through the boundaries imposed by circumstances. Even a cursory examination reveals the 'realism' of the Dutch to be a skilful illusion. A Frans Hals portrait is as impressionist in its technique as a Van Gogh. Even the cows in a Cuyp rural scene, meticulously accurate though they are, achieve a grouping so harmonious and satisfying that it meets every demand that the critic can make upon it – whether of form, balance or tactile values. The crudity of the subject-matter of Jan Steen or Brouwer cannot conceal the superlative technique and inspiration that mould the composition into impressive coherence. Above all towers the achievement of Rembrandt himself – brooding, mysterious, miraculously penetrating in his apprehension of nature and man. Again, an audacity of line and colour that lifts portraits, biblical scenes and sketches of domestic life clean out of locality and period. The self-portraits, combining nobility, comedy, tragedy, grotesquerie, remain one of the greatest achievements of the creative human genius.

The Trips were one of the richest merchant dynasties of Holland. With the De Geers they virtually monopolised the Baltic trades in corn, salt, copper, tar and arms. While one branch moved to Amsterdam, Jacob (1575–1661) stayed at Dordrecht. The Trips gave Rembrandt four commissions, including this portrait of Jacob and two of his wife Margaretha (*nee* De Geer), as well as others to Nicolas Maes and J.G.Cuyp. London, National Gallery.

As Calvinism deprived the painters of religious themes of much of their patronage, the commissions from wealthy corporations grew in value. Among the greatest in this genre is Rembrandt's *Syndics of the Cloth Makers of Amsterdam*, where the artist brings what might have been a stiff and formal group to dramatic life. Rijksmuseum, Amsterdam.

Sometimes an artist went too far for contemporary taste in suppressing the purely descriptive or dramatic element with which clients liked to celebrate a scene in their town, a storm at sea or a rain shower drifting across a distant landscape pursued by sunshine. Vermeer's *Girl with the Pearl Earrings* was sold in the 1880s in an auction in Holland for four shillings. The rediscovery of Vermeer was largely due to the Impressionists and it was not accidental. The Dutch, like the Impressionists, were masters of light. As Paul Zumthor says, 'The most genuinely lyrical form taken by Dutch painting of the era was the landscape, with the chiaroscuro inspired by the vast expanse of the Dutch sky'. [26] Light gave to the Dutch artist a subtlety that replaced the extrovert, passionate drama, human or natural, of the Italians. In Vermeer (as sometimes in Rembrandt) the human drama is muted. There is a quality of brooding stillness. Even hands that write, sew or simply hold often seem like objects in a still life.

Beerstraten's characteristic winter scene at the castle of Muiden on the Zuiderzee has interest beyond its qualities as a landscape painting. The castle was the meeting place of the 'Muiderkring', a circle of Dutch humanists, historians, poets and scholars who played an important part in opposing Calvinist bigotry and promoting intellectual freedom. National Gallery, London. (Detail.)

The continuing popularity and influence of the Dutch school has rested on this unique combination of technical mastery and intense artistic vision. It spread most rapidly and took root most deeply where economic and geographical circumstances were most favourable and where artists experienced natural conditions of landscape and light similar to those in which the Dutch had themselves worked. Such conditions existed across the North Sea in England.

Artists from those parts of England which had most affinities with Holland – East Anglia – remained most susceptible to the spell of Hobbema and Van de Capelle. To them, the North Sea was not so much a barrier as a highway linking two worlds which had much in common.

These were later flowerings. The two centuries which produced some of the greatest of English poetry, prose, drama and music, showed little spontaneity in visual art. Even war and religious upheaval can hardly account for the absence of great painting in Tudor England. The lavish patronage of the Stuart courts, and the growing demand for portrait painting, only served to emphasise the lack of native talent. Daniel Mytens, Paul van Somer, Cornelius Johnson, Gerad Soest, Marc Gheeraerdts, Pieter Borsseler, Abraham van Diepenbeke, the Van de Veldes, Peter Lely – these are the names which go to make up the 'English' school of seventeenth-century painters. Yet they are all Flemish or Dutch artists who were attracted to England by the promise of handsome patronage between 1600 and 1680. Inevitably they are overshadowed by Van Dyck, who settled in London as court painter in 1632 and who was to dominate English portrait painting for a century and a half.

Even before his arrival, there were already two Netherlands painters of some stature working in England. Daniel Mytens was a Dutch pupil of Rubens who was appointed court painter to

James I. Mytens was a gifted painter whose work ranged between the literalness of his Dutch contemporaries and the fuller magnificence of Van Dyck; his portrait of Charles I is in the first manner, his *James, Second Marquess of Hamilton* in the second. Cornelius Johnson, the son of a Fleming, was born in London, and during his English period his work has a good deal in common with Van Dyck's. Both Mytens and Johnson returned to Holland in later years, concious, no doubt, they were being overshadowed by the genius of Van Dyck and Lely. With the appointment of Van Dyck to the court in 1632, a new era opened in English painting. No artist has ever infused into the painting of English men and women the character of an age and society as did the Netherlander Van Dyck. Or was it the other way round – was it Van Dyck's genius which helped to create the 'Cavalier' legend? It is interesting to speculate how our conception of the Stuart age has been shaped by Van Dyck and his Dutch successor, Lely, as well as by that attractive impostor of Hals *The Laughing Cavalier* who presumably owes his English reputation to a characteristic English illusion that Dutch artists only painted Englishmen. No English artist appeared to immortalise the Cavalier except William Dobson, and he too was a pupil of Van Dyck. Even Robert Walker, the Puritan painter of Puritans, of Cromwell and Hampden, followed the Van Dyck manner.

The later years of the Republican period and the Restoration were dominated by another Dutch artist, Sir Peter Lely, a pupil of De Grebber of Haarlem, who came over in 1641 in the train of William, Prince of Orange; the occasion was William's marriage to Charles I's daughter Mary, and Lely's portraits of the bridal couple helped to establish his reputation, bringing him customers galore. Lely quickly adapted himself to the Van Dyck tradition – so adroitly that some of his portraits have been ascribed to Van Dyck. His best known works are comprised in the *Flagmen* collection in the

Maritime Museum at Greenwich, and in the *Windsor Beauties* at Hampton Court. The latter – especially the portraits of Lady Byrom and Lady Falmouth – have been held to set Lely apart as a colourist and portrait painter. Yet as a collection *The Beauties* fall short of the uniform perfection of the *Flagmen* portraits. In his diary for 18 April 1666, Pepys writes:

> To Mr Lilly's, the painters, and there saw the heads – some finished and all begun – of the flagg-men in the late great fight with the Duke of York against the Dutch. The Duke of York hath them done to hang in his Chamber, and very finely they are done indeed. Here are the Prince's [Rupert's], Sir George Askue's, Sir Thomas Teddiman's, Sir Christopher Ming's, Sir Joseph Jorden, Sir William Berkeley, Sir Thomas Allen, and Captain Harman's, as also the Duke of Albemarle's; and will be my Lord Sandwich's, Sir W. Penn's and Sir Jeremy Smith's,[27]

If it is odd that we should owe our image of the English Cavalier partly to a Fleming, it is no less curious that the finest portrait of a seventeenth-century English admiral – the dour Sir Jeremy Smith on which the paint was not yet dry when Pepys saw it – should have been painted by a Dutchman. Yet it was typical of the age that neither sitter nor artist should have felt any embarrassment on the political count. Perhaps it was his Dutch training that enabled Lely to adapt himself to the sombre mood of the Flagmen more easily than to the contemporary tastes of the court in female beauty.

Gerard Soest, the painter of the famous *Aubrey de Vere, Earl of Oxford* (in the Dulwich Gallery) was another Dutchman who came to England about the same time as Lely; if not a pupil of Lely's, his work is certainly in the Van Dyck-Lely tradition. A later (and lesser) arrival, Jacob Huysmans, the Antwerper, enjoyed a considerable reputation for a time, and was considered by some 'to exceed Lilly'.

By 1680, when Lely died, a few English artists were beginning to

Portrait of Cardinal Richelieu, by Philippe de Champaigne (1602–74). Some Netherlands painters emigrated in search of lucrative contracts at the courts of Europe. Champaigne, born in Brussels, was one such; he settled in Paris in 1621 to work for Marie de Medicis. National Gallery, London.

appear – notably John Riley, a pupil of Soest and later of Lely, and John Greenhill. But the greatest figure was still that of the foreigner – a German it is true, but Dutch by training and tradition. Sir Godfrey Kneller studied in Holland, probably with the great Ferdinand Bol. With Kneller we come to the establishment of a school of English portrait painting; the Dutch names became fewer.

Van Dyck, Lely, Mytens, Soest – these are the greatest names, but there were many other lesser men who worked in England – Adrian Hanneman of the Hague, Abraham Hondius of Rotterdam, Isakk Luttichuys of Amsterdam, Gerard Edema, 'court painter' (as it were) to Lord Mountedgcumbe and deviser of great romantic landscapes and tropical scenes, and many more. The portrait painters were not the only artists to be attracted by the generous royal and aristocratic patronage which England offered. The painters of seascapes and landscapes were also well represented. Of the former, the most prolific and famous were undoubtedly the Van de Veldes, appointed to the court by the special charter of Charles II in 1676. They rivalled the greatness of Lely's admirals in their paintings of sea scenes and naval battles and their *grisaille* drawings of ships. Among the landscape painters were Josse de Momper, David Vinckeboons, Francis Cleyn and Thomas Wyck, who specialised in views of London.

The French school of realist painters also had close, in some cases, specific links with the Dutch school. A group that includes Le Nain, Eustache Le Sueur and – greatest of all – Philippe de Champaigne, thought in terms very similar to those of their Dutch contemporaries. De Champaigne indeed was a Fleming, born in Brussels. Other Netherlands painters who were attracted to France included Kalff, Bloemaert, and Pijnacker who worked in Paris, Van der Kabel at Lyons.

With the eighteenth century came a rapid decline in the quality

of art in the Netherlands, a decline that was reflected in a reduction in the number of Dutch artists working in England. A handful of painters and sculptors (like Scheemakers, Rysbrach and Van Nost) was still to be found, but the time of Dutch preponderance was over. The influence of the Netherlands school, however, was undiminished. Van Dyck and Lely remained the giants of the world of portraiture; even Hogarth, though affecting to despise the imitators of foreign fashions, learnt much from the realism of Jan Steen and Ostade. But most remarkable was the gradual unfolding in the eastern counties of a style of landscape painting which owed at any rate its beginnings to the study of the Dutch masters – of Cuyp, Hobbema, and Ruysdael.

The artist of East Anglia shared with the Dutch masters a flat or gently undulating landscape that did not lend itself to heroics: this – often regarded as dull country – was the home of most of the best

English landscape painters; more dramatic scenery has only gladdened a thousand Victorian back-parlours with *The Highland Glen* and *A Stag at Bay*. The native scene of Gainsborough, Crome and Constable was a land of windmills, locks and waterways, creeks and inlets and sea views. Not only the homely and pastoral subjects, but conditions of atmosphere and light were very similar in both countries. That permanent April state, where darkening clouds forever threaten a fugitive sunshine, was nature's gift to a race of artists whose genius lay above all in the study of light. The early landscapes of Gainsborough (a Suffolk man) were strongly influenced by the works of Jan Wynants and other minor Dutch artists whose pictures were frequently to be found in private collections in East Anglian houses. John Constable, another East Anglian, was (as his pictures so often remind us) the son of a miller who owned both windmills and watermills. But it is John Crome who reminds us most vividly how close eastern England is to Holland; yet at the same time he manages to achieve a sense of local and purely English atmosphere which bears comparison with the achievements of Hobbema, Ruysdael or the Vermeer of the *View of Delft*. Whether it is the windmill and sails of his *Moonrise on the Yare* (reminiscent of Van der Neer) or the ships in his *Yarmouth Harbour* (which owed much to Albert Cuyp) or the tawny sails of his last picture *Yarmouth Water Frolic*, here is an artist who was intimately linked not only in technique but in temper with the great Dutch masters of the seventeenth century.

One cannot help wondering whether Crome had any connections with the Dutch colonies of Norwich or Colchester, or at any rate whether it was perhaps through some of the wealthier Dutch settlers that the eastern counties were introduced to Dutch art. There is evidence of the same influence though in a lesser degree in other artists – in Cotman, Bonington, even in Turner. In each case, however, the Dutch tradition was absorbed and adapted into a

The Norwich school is the most striking example of a large group of painters directly influenced by the Dutch example. John Crome (1768–1821) was a leading figure, as shown by his *Moonrise on the Yare*. It was not only geographical proximity and similarity of light and climate which made for this link; barley and cloth could provide patronage comparable to that which sustained artists in Haarlem or Amsterdam. Tate Gallery, London.

new and unmistakably local synthesis. There was no mere slavish imitation, though occasionally the literalness which suited a Hobbema or a Ruysdael became a handicap to lesser men. The Dutch model was what a model should be – a stimulus to be like but different; allowing a wide scope for local variation yet near enough in subject and temper to provide an attainable ideal. The example of Hobbema, Cuyp, Ruysdael was an indispensable element in the formation of an original and characteristically English school of landscape painting in the eighteenth century: yet all the time, the English painters were moving away from realism to impressionism. Crome – Constable – Turner, each represents a step in a typically English process of assimilation and change. Here, long after the great Dutchmen had gone, the Dutch genius lived on in new forms: the story goes that Gainsborough died as he had lived speaking of Van Dyck, that John Crome died with Hobbema's name on his lips.

Thus, even when the richest period of creation was over, Dutch influences lived on. The Dutch school had brought into painting not only new subject-matter but a realistic concept of landscape and a sense of the picturesque to which painters, French as well as English, Fragonard and Boilly as well as Crome and Gainsborough, owed a great deal. To speak of Courbet is to think of Rembrandt. The new humanism of the Dutch artists made of the 'golden century' one of the greatest moments in the history of painting.

Flemish and Dutch influences on architecture were hardly less pronounced than on painting during the last decade of the sixteenth and the first half of the seventeenth century. In East Anglia especially, the stepped and curled gables (introduced first possibly by the immigrant weavers from the Low Countries in their own houses and cottages) became a native style; the hall at Fen Ditton, the cottages at Fen Stanton and Fen Drayton, the 'White Hart' at Scole, the Fishermen's Almshouses at Yarmouth, and Raynham Hall are examples of the 'social' variety of the Dutch style. The fashion was not so lasting in its architectural as in its artistic phase, perhaps because, while the painters of the northern Netherlands were emancipating themselves from Italian influences in this period, the architects, there as in England, were falling more and more under classical influences.

One of the valuable contributions made by the Dutch architects and writers of text-books of this period was to transmit to England scale-drawings of the designs of the Italian masters – of Serlio, Vignola and Palladio. For while the Dutch style in painting was becoming more and more characteristic, Dutch architecture was

Overleaf: As Dutch traders linked the Mediterranean and the Baltic, so artists travelled north as well as south. Allaert van Everdingen (1621–75) sailed to Norway and Sweden, and the coniferous forests and waterfalls figure in this *Swedish Landscape* much as the traditional Tuscan valleys had dominated earlier generations of painters. Rijksmuseum, Amsterdam.

steadily absorbing more southern influence as time went on, and indeed is often merged and lost in the comprehensive term 'Palladianism'. In fact, Dutch architecture retained several important distinctive features which were taken over by the English architects of the late seventeenth and early eighteenth centuries, and embodied in the Georgian style.

Some of the architects who did much to popularise Netherlandish fashions in English design were themselves Flemish or Dutch; others were Englishmen who had learned from Dutch craftsmen or Dutch text-books. Amongst the immigrant designers were Casper Vosbergh, who worked for Cecil at Burghley House, Stamford; Henry de Pas, who is credited with the design of Sir Thomas Gresham's Exchange (Gresham's own life-story is symbolic of the close economic relations existing between the two countries in Tudor times when, as often later, England's war potential was drawn from over the sea); and Bernard Jansen, who was largely responsible for Audley End. More shadowy but not less interesting, was 'the ingenious and learned Captain Wynne' (or Winde), a native of Bergen-op-Zoom, the designer of Hamstead Marshall (now destroyed), Newcastle House, Lincoln's Inn Fields, and old Buckingham House. (Wynne's original drawings for Hamstead Marshall are still in the Bodleian.)

The continual flow of craftsmen and ideas from the Netherlands reached its climax in the early seventeenth century, the period when Dutch ideas – curled gables and scrolls, strapwork and the extensive use of brickwork – were at the height of their popularity. Especially during the middle years of Charles I's reign, the number of houses, town residences as well as country mansions, in the 'Dutch gable' style, multiplied. Raynham Hall, Norfolk, with its smooth brickwork, stone quoins and dressings, is a typical and magnificent example. Others like Broome Park, Kent (1635) and Swakeleys, Middlesex (1638), have wooden mullions. Lilford Hall,

De Bevrs
La Bourse

Northamptonshire, belongs to the same period and style, as does Ashdown House, Berkshire (built by John Webb, nephew and pupil of Inigo Jones, for the first Lord Craven) which still towers over the Berkshire Downs. Amsterdam House, at Christchurch, Hampshire, built of bricks specially imported from the Netherlands, was unfortunately pulled down some years ago.

In London itself, there were a number of houses in the Dutch style, one attractive example being the house we today call Kew Palace. The original house on the site was bought in 1630 from a Dutch merchant by another Dutchman, Samuel Fortrey (well known as a writer on economic affairs) who pulled it down and built the present house in the following year. Kew Palace has most of the usual features of the Dutch style – the carved gables and fine brickwork in Flemish bond – and both the palace and the nearby cottage (also in the same style) are enhanced by their magnificent setting. In this way they were more fortunate than Schomberg House in Pall Mall, an example of the later Dutch style, classical in mood but still showing a good deal of Dutch influence in the elevation, which was built for the Duke in 1698.

Interior design reflects the same trend. Elaborate and sometimes hideous chimney pieces were copied from Flemish examples, of which a good specimen may be found at Knole, Kent. The popularity of Delft tiles has been touched on elsewhere. When Marlborough House was being built, Wren wrote to Sarah to say that 12,000 Dutch tiles would be needed for the rooms, and about 2,200 for the chimneys (31 October 1710). Possibly Marlborough may have turned a returning supply ship to good account to meet the occasion. At the Queen's House, Greenwich, blue and white Delft tiles formed a dado in one of the rooms.

What of the future? The period which lies between the Glorious Revolution and, say, 1747 (when the tax on mahogany was lifted) was the age of walnut in England: it was also a time when English conceptions of domestic comfort and convenience underwent a rapid change. A typical house of 1690 or 1700 would contain many pieces of furniture previously unknown in England – china cabinets for the new Delft or oriental wares, mirrors in veneered frames surrounded by floral designs in rich marquetry in the manner of Van Huysum, a long-case clock veneered with marquetry, writing

cabinets, washstands and tallboys, and lacquered furniture in imitation of the Chinese work imported by the Dutch East India Company. There would probably be a suite of furniture, designed by Daniel Marot, the Huguenot refugee who came over in the service of William and Mary and the greatest of the foreign craftsmen working in England (if we exclude Grinling Gibbons). There would be chairs richly upholstered in velvet or in tapestry worked by the Flemings of Mortlake, who were induced to settle there by James I and survived throughout the walnut period. Most of these fashions in walnut were borrowed from so many other sources – French, Spanish, and oriental – that to identify and distinguish is often difficult if not impossible.

Meanwhile the English craftsman was rapidly becoming proficient in these imported fashions and was soon successfully cutting and laying veneers with and without marquetry, and imitating the lacquered magnificence of his foreign rival. He learnt, too, new methods of construction from the Dutch craftsmen. Screws and lapped dovetail joints replaced the Birmingham nail that had served well enough for the old days of oak but was necessarily ousted from the new and more refined world of highly-polished and figured surfaces: he learnt to cut his timber at such an angle as to obtain the richest effects from the tones and lines of the grain; even knots and burrs were cut so as to provide patterned veneers of the greatest beauty. Above all, he learnt to turn a cabriole leg – probably a form of ancient oriental origin – which began its long period of popularity about this time. In short it was during these years, with their astonishing and sometimes garish variety of styles, that the English craftsman learned to assimilate many of the methods and designs which were later incorporated in the work of his great successors in the age of Chippendale, Hepplewhite and Sheraton.

In the same period the Dutch garden, with its high, thick, clipped yew hedges and box trees curling into fantastic shapes – heraldic beasts, ships and even biblical tableaux – became so fashionable that it was in the end killed by its own extravagance. The geometrical precision of the Dutch style did not, it must be confessed, really fit the English scene, and the visitor to Levens Hall, Westmorland, will probably sympathise with the *Spectator* when it wrote:

Our trees rise in Cones, Globes and Pyramids. We see the Marks of the Scissors upon every Plant and Bush. I do not know whether I am singular in my opinion, but, for my own part, I would rather look upon a Tree in all its Luxuriancy and Diffusion of Boughs and Branches than when it is thus cut and trimmed into a Mathematical Figure.

The 'Cabbage' rose (or Batavian rose as it was called) seems to have been almost extinct in western Europe in the Middle Ages. It reappeared in the Netherlands in the last century when it was

What Pieter Breughel had done for the Flemish peasant, Jan Steen, Adriaen Brouwer and his friend Adriaen van Ostade did for the urban and rural poor in the north. Watercolour in the British Museum, London.

commented on by the great Dutch botanist Clusius. Apparently it was not commonly grown until the second quarter of the next century: as its popularity grew we find it appearing occasionally in the paintings of Justus van Huysum, and regularly and indubitably in those of his son Jan van Huysum, the greatest of the Dutch flower painters. Where it came from it is hard to say; possibly it was brought back from the Levant by one of the many Dutch traders there. At any rate, it was certainly from the Netherlands that it was introduced into England and France.

The pattern of the formal Dutch style, with its coloured gravels and its brass and lead statues, was nicely calculated to eke out the cramped plots behind the great houses by the canals of the Dutch towns; imposed on the spacious and natural beauty of English park land, it was apt to become a horticultural strait-jacket. The best examples of the Dutch styles are Wrest Park (Bedfordshire), Melbourne (Derbyshire) – both adorned with Van Nost's work – and Hampton Court.

The popularity of the Dutch style in architecture, at any rate in its most obvious and characteristic form as at Kew Palace or Raynham, was shortlived. Other styles, chiefly Italian and French, soon toned down its native originality and we must look closely to discern its continuing influence in more subtle forms in the work of Christopher Wren and his followers. Wren travelled abroad very little. But that did not mean he was insulated from foreign influence. He had upon his shelves a number of folios into which contemporary Dutch writers on architecture had concentrated the essentials of Renaissance design and experience. In 1641 his friend John Evelyn, the diarist, visited the Amsterdam shop of Hondius and Blaeu, buying books and maps of Serlio and Vignola. Serlio's *Bookes of Architecture* were first translated from Italian into Dutch and later, in 1611, from Dutch into English.

In 1631 Cornelius Danckerts de Rij published his *Architectura*

Moderna containing many of Hendrik de Keyser's works at Amsterdam. Bloem's *Boek van de Vijf Columnen van Architecture*, which was already in existence, was in Evelyn's collection. Hendrik Hondius's own *Les Cinq Rangs de L'Architecture* had appeared in Amsterdam in 1617. All these books contained scale drawings and were probably known to Wren.

The most influential drawings were the works of Philip Vingboons. His designs for town houses of the kind which may still be seen along the canals of Amsterdam, such as the great house built for Trips, the bankers, in 1662, undoubtedly influenced Wren. They helped to bring to maturity the style we call the Georgian Vernacular, the most typically English of architectual styles. At the same time the designs of Jacob van Campen, the architect of the Royal Palace at Amsterdam, in the manner of Palladio and Scamozzi, were being published. Other ideas which Wren probably borrowed from Holland were the sash window (which was well-known there early in the century) and the combination of broad surfaces of brick with stone quoins. Returning prosperity in England in the post-Restoration period made it a lively place for

In 1641 the diarist John Evelyn visited Amsterdam and bought a number of books by Dutch draughtsmen reproducing Italian architectural designs. Dutch architects themselves had already incorporated classical designs into their work. This drawing by Danckert of Amsterdam gate towers (*left*) is echoed in Wren's design for St Bride's steeple, Fleet Street, London (*right*).

architects and builders. So did the need to rebuild London after the Great Fire of 1666. Much of the new work replaced the old, insanitary and inflammable lath-and-plaster houses by brick. Naturally, the builders turned to the masters of brick building, the Dutch, for ideas and materials. Architectural borrowings were not limited to domestic architecture. Medieval English church building could show no precedent for the Wren steeples, with their mounting stages of concave and convex ornament, but they have their antecedents in earlier Dutch spires such as the Zuiderkerk and the Westertoren at Amsterdam. Wren may well have assimilated at least some of these ideas from the designs of Danckert and Hondius, for it was a mark of his greatness that he was able to draw on the experience of others and make of it something specially suited to the English scene, the English temperament, and the English climate. By 1688 Wren had helped to fuse some of the best elements of Dutch and English design. Thereafter, the lines of architectural development in England and Holland were to run parallel.

8 An exchange of letters

The coming of the new Europe and the formation of national states did not extinguish immediately the cosmopolitan spirit of the Middle Ages. Among scholars and men of letters it lived on. England and the Netherlands offered hospitality to each other's scholars even when the struggle for commercial and maritime supremacy was at its most bitter. Authors and artists moved from one country to the other as easily as from Kent to Surrey. A hundred years after Erasmus of Rotterdam kept at Queens' College, Cambridge, for the last time, there were Dutch canons at Canterbury and Windsor, English, Scottish and French professors and students at Amsterdam and Leyden, Dutch painters at the English court, English poets and philosophers at Amsterdam and the Hague. The obstacles of distance and language were overcome or ignored. Even Anglo-Dutch wars did little to disturb these colonies.

Some of the emigrants were refugees but there were many voluntary exiles: and in those days of leisured, casual diplomacy, it was natural that many of those who mingled and enriched the literature of both countries should have been ambassadors or diplomatists. Towards the end of the sixteenth century, for example, Dirk (Theodore) Rodenburgh, the Dutch poet and dramatist, visited England as an emissary of the Dutch government, and came under the influence of the Elizabethan dramatists. Rodenburgh translated Sidney's *Apologie for Poetrie* and Cyril Tourneur's *Revenger's Tragedy* into Dutch. In 1600 the Pensionary Jacob Cats visited England for the first time, going to Cambridge and Oxford. Cats was no mere rustic wit: he was a man of wide culture, a capable jurist and a tolerably good administrator. Constantijn Huygens – diplomat, administrator and poet – also came frequently to England on official errands and was the friend of John Donne. His own verse was considerably influenced by the example of the English 'metaphysicals'. Since the year of the Armada, when Elizabeth decided to support the rebels, the Huygens family were

Constantijn Huygens (1596–1687) was Secretary to the Stadholder, Frederick Henry, when De Keyser painted this portrait of him in 1627. His wide interests are symbolised by the lute, terrestrial globes, book, compasses and quill-pen and ink. Boots and spurs mark his knighthood by James I five years earlier. National Gallery, London.

on friendly terms with a succession of English diplomats: Thomas Bodley, founder of the Bodleian Library at Oxford, was one, Sir Henry Wotton, ambassador to Holland and a friend of Donne, another. Through such friends Constantijn came to visit Oxford and Cambridge, to stay at the great new palace at Audley End, to be familiar at court. (He was knighted in 1622.)

Another important Dutch figure in London was Emanuel van Meteren, originally born an Antwerper, friend of Ortelius the map-maker, who had emigrated first to Holland and then to London. Van Meteren was a merchant and a keen collector and bibliophile too. He was the friend and correspondent of distinguished Dutch families (including the Huygens) and the centre of much diplomatic activity in London. Later he wrote the history of the Dutch revolt which remains an important source of historical information. His comments on the English are as frank as they are enlightening. The men were 'clever, handsome but . . . weak and tender'; courteous, indolent, hospitable and hypocritical; 'stout-hearted, vehement, eager, cruel in war, zealous in attack, little fearing death, not vindictive but fickle, presumptuous, casual and elusive . . . very suspicious of strangers, whom they despise'.

From the English side, Christopher Marlowe, Ben Johnson, Giles Fletcher and John Donne all visited the Low Countries. Milton never did, as far as is known, though he had close contacts there. He did however visit Grotius, now in exile in Paris, in 1638, and was 'kindly received'. Milton's *Paradise Lost* may owe something to Grotius's Latin poem *Adamus Exul* (1601). And an intriguing literary triangle is formed by the great religious epic poem *Lucifer* by the Dutch poet, Joost van den Vondel. More than one critical eyebrow has been raised at the strong resemblances, even in detail, between Milton's epic and the earlier Dutch poem. Was Milton a plagiarist? The problem is insoluble. What is certain is that Milton, Vondel – and indeed Grotius – all used the same theme. All

Joost van den Vondel was the greatest poet of the Dutch golden age. He rejected the Calvinist doctrine of predestination as a barbarous slur on man's capacity for free decision. A humanist and the friend of humanists, he died a Catholic.

were humanists, all were opposed to what they regarded as the repulsive and brutalising doctrine of predestination. In all three poems the argument ran that man was afforded the means of salvation from a state of sin which was itself the result of the exercise of his own free will.

This common concern with the issue of free will was not accidental. Grotius had been the protector and friend of Vondel in Holland. Vondel had dedicated his tragedy *Gijsbrecht/van Amstel* to Grotius. Both had been friends and supporters of the Grand Pensionary, Oldenbarneveldt, in the fight against the extreme Calvinists that ended in Oldenbarneveldt's execution. Vondel was the friend of Gerard Vossius, a leader of the moderate Dutch Arminians. Through Archbishop Laud (and probably with the help of the learned and saintly Lancelot Andrews, Bishop of Winchester) Vossius became a canon of Canterbury. (His son, Isaac, also a great if eccentric scholar, became a canon of Windsor.) Vossius was brother-in-law of another learned Dutch antiquarian, Francis

Junius, of Leyden. Through another Anglican bishop, Ussher, Junius came into possession of the manuscript of the so-called 'Caedmon' poems, paraphrases of the Old Testament. His researches were certainly available to Milton. The existence of this influential group of humanist, sometimes Arminian, Churchmen and scholars suggests that the important issue here is not plagiarism, but a deeply felt antipathy, common to Dutch and English humanism alike, to Calvinist theology in its extreme form.

In the more secular phase that followed Charles II's Restoration in 1660, Sir William Temple was active in stimulating Dutch interest in English writing while he was minister to the States General. His essay *Of Poetry* seems to have commanded as wide a public in the Netherlands as his *Observations on the United Provinces* did in England. Temple's mission was carried on by the Whig exiles, by Burnet, the confidant and adviser of both William and Mary, by the Earl of Shaftesbury, and by John Locke. From 1684 to 1688 Locke lived at Amsterdam and Utrecht, presiding precariously (as Mynheer van der Linden) over his Lantern Club, and periodically fleeing extradition along the alleys and canals of the Dutch cities. The diplomat replaced the refugee once more in the person of Matthew Prior, who became secretary to William the Third's ambassador at the Hague, and an Interim Gentleman of the Bedchamber to the king. Prior once described himself, as 'only a poet by accident'. It is true that he was also a diligent and by no means unsuccessful diplomat – witness his part in the negotiations leading up to the Treaty of Ryswick; while

> In the vile Utrecht Treaty, too,
> Poor man! He found enough to do.[28]

But besides being part-author of what was sometimes called 'Matt's Peace', Prior was also a witty and delightful lyric poet. His poem *The Secretary*, in which he describes the pleasure of life at the Hague, atones in some measure for Andrew Marvell's rudeness:

> With labour assiduous due pleasure I mix,
> And in one day atone for the business of six
> In a little Dutch chaise, on a Saturday night,
> On my left hand my Horace, a nymph on my right;
> No memoirs to compose, and no post-boy to move,
> That on Sunday may hinder the softness of love;
> For her, neither visits, nor parties at tea,
> Nor the long-winded cant of a dull refugee:
> This night and the next shall be hers, shall be mine;
> To good or ill-fortune the third we resign.
> Thus scorning the world, and Superior to Fate
> I drive my car in professional state;
> So with Phia thro' Athens Pisistratus rode,
> Men thought her Minerva and him a new God.
> But why should I stories of Athens rehearse,
> Where people knew love and were partial to verse,
> Since none can with justice my pleasures oppose
> In Holland half-drowned in int'rest and prose?
> By Greece and past ages what need I be tried
> When the Hague and the present are both by my side?
> And is it enough for the joys of the day
> To think what Anacreon or Sappho would say,
> When good Vandergoes and his provident Vrouw,
> As they gaze on my triumph, so freely allow,
> That search all the Province, you'll find no man dar is,
> So blest as the *Englishen Heer Secretar* is?

By 1700 continuous interchange had created intelligent interest among the Dutch reading public in English writing and in the potentialities of the English language as a medium of expression. This interest was stimulated by the great printing and book-selling trade which had grown up in seventeenth-century Holland, where Blaeu produced the first great technological advance in printing since the machines of Gutenberg. Many famous English works, both verse and prose, were first printed there. Milton, Thomas Browne, and many others had their works printed at Amsterdam and Leyden, sometimes in Dutch as well as in English versions. This is the period of the pocket classics produced by the Elzevir Press, while many of our best surviving quartos and folios of the period were published by Janssen, Blaeu or Plantin at Amsterdam, Leyden and Utrecht. The pre-eminence of Amsterdam in printing and book-selling was itself largely the result of her geographical and economic position.

By 1700 the culture of the Republic had lost much of its originality and vitality partly by reason of the continual traffic in foreign ideas and fashions. Even while Holland was at war with France, the Dutch intelligentsia showed itself as anxious to absorb or affect French literary fashions as the gallants of Dutch society were to ape, in ludicrous detail, the mannerisms of Versailles.

What had England to offer? She had, of course, the poets and dramatists of the Elizabethan, Jacobean and Restoration periods; she had Milton and the Metaphysicals. These were known and admired in Holland. There were English strolling players, who seem to have attracted a large following less through their speech (which was largely unintelligible to a Dutch audience) than through their sex-appeal, which caused some local feeling . . .

the people not understanding what they sayd, only for theire Action followed them with wonderfull concourse, yea many young Virgines fell in love with some of the players, and followed them from Citty to Citty, till the Magistrates were forced to forbid them to play any more.[29]

Prose was more to the Dutchman's taste than poetry, and philosophy more popular than the drama. (Amsterdam had no theatre except an occasional booth set up by travelling actors at the fair.) Above all, the Dutch admired English 'social' literature – the journals and broadsheets of London's coffee-houses and literary cliques. This literary life was itself symbolic of an important social change in England, where literature, philosophy and decent manners were ceasing to be the exclusive property of a small minority of educated people. The champions of taste and respectability were drawing together – from the merchants and bankers of the City, from the universities and even the Church and the sects: the London of Johnson's day (which he maintained was the most civilised city in the world) was steadily taking shape. There was conscious effort to achieve standards of taste and conduct, to brush under the carpet the boorishness of rustic England, the immorality of the Court, the drunkenness and dirt that festered in Gin Alley: in short, to try and make a world fit for the respectable brewers and bankers who were to be the patrons of Johnson, Garrick and Reynolds.

As yet the attack on manners was directed by the satirist rather than the preacher. Society had had its fill of Restoration pleasure, but there were still enough people alive who remembered stories of the major-generals to fight shy of correction from the pulpit. Until the time of Whitefield and Wesley, the way of salvation was not to be made too narrow. Philosophers exalted the classical virtues, the coffee-houses buzzed with the astringent malice of wit against wit, the theatre entered upon a period of classical moderation. The actress, her ambition no longer limited to the dubious honour of becoming the mistress of the rake or the gallant, might aspire to be the companion of the philosopher and the artist. The chief missionary in this campaign to refine and civilise society was the *Spectator*, which said of itself that it 'brought philosophy out of the closets and libraries, schools and colleges to dwell in clubs and Assemblies, at Tea Tables and in Coffee Houses'.[30]

The *Spectator* had an irresistible appeal in Holland. The peak of Dutch commercial prosperity coincided with a decline of literary genius and a mania for the appearances of French style and

Justus van Effen, whose Dutch equivalent of Addison's *Spectator* followed his English model closely and professed the same aim of moral and social improvement.

manners. This produced no native writing of any merit and threatened to stifle what local talent still remained. A reaction was inevitable, and it came in the person of Justus van Effen, of Utrecht. Van Effen was educated at Utrecht University, and first came to England in 1715 as an under-secretary at the Embassy. In the same year he was made a member of the Royal Society and met Newton, Pope and Swift. Later he returned to Holland and worked at Leyden University. In 1727 he came back to England as secretary to an old pupil who represented Holland at the coronation of George II – an event which Van Effen celebrated in verse.

The early papers for which Van Effen was largely responsible – the *Misantrope* and the *Bagatelle* – were written in French, although they bear the mark of his stay in England; and he was already borrowing from Addison and Steele. Like them, Van Effen attacked what he considered were the worst of the current

No. 3.

Den 3. September 1731.

DE
HOLLANDSCHE
SPECTATOR.

Qui Bavium non odit , amet tua carmina Mævi.

VIRG.

Nlangs heb ik by geval 't geluk gehad van kennis te maaken met een fatzoenlyk Burgerman , die, hoewel zyne levenswyze zich laagjens by de grond houd, veel geld, door zyn naarstigheid en goed overleg verkregen, bezit. My dunkt dat by alle Volken het middelbare slag van Menschen het beste is, en zulks meen ik wel voornamentlyk in onze landaard te hebben ondervonden. Ik wil gaaren bekennen dat ik met diergelyke lieden het liefst omga. Myn nieuwe Vriend is niet openhartig, rondborstig, oprecht; 't is de oprechtheid en openhartigheid zelfs. Niets kan goedaardiger en vriendhoudender uitgedacht worden; in zyn leedige uuren is men hem altyd welkom , voornamentlyk indien men voor een verstandig of geestryk man te boek staat. 't Is echter geen man van studie, maar in zaaken; waar op hy gevat is, en in welke zyne reden, door een al te groote onderwerping aan 't gevoelen van anderen niet misleid word, van een

C

zeer

vices – debauchery, duelling, atheism and ignorance – and exalted education and the social virtues. By the time he came to write the *Holandsche Spectator*, his ideas had crystallised and his judgment had hardened against those French influences by which his earlier work and style had been shaped. He now wrote quite deliberately in his own language in defiance of polite convention. Nevertheless, it is symptomatic of the dilemma of his countrymen, caught in the prevailing European cross-currents, that Van Effen, in order to eject the French devil, had to introduce the English. Van Effen kept his eye steadily on his ultimate object – to purge Dutch society of foreign fopperies and affectations which threatened to make the educated Dutchman look absurd, to encourage his countrymen to a confidence in themselves and their own native culture, and to shape a Dutch prose style comparable with the flowing measure of his English models.

The *Hollandsche Spectator*, which ran from 20 August 1731 to 8 April 1735, was modelled very closely on its English namesake, as Van Effen acknowledged frankly in the first number. 'The English work which I propose not to translate but to imitate in my mother tongue . . .'

For the most part, he tilted at the same sort of victim as Addison and Steele; for society in Holland had not changed much since the seventeenth century, and the scenes that inspired Jan Steen provoked Van Effen in much the same way as the London of Hogarth provoked Addison. Yet there was a difference. It was Owen Feltham who had described the Dutch 'drinking down the Evening Starre and drinking up the Morning Starre'. Sir Thomas Overburry repeated the charge: 'Concerning the people: they are neither much devout, nor much wicked; given all to drink, and eminently to no other vice: hard in bargaining, but just; surly and respectless, as in all democracies; thirsty, industrious and cleanly –' and so on. There was, however, one important change since the riper, lustier days of Tromp and De Ruyter, Jan Steen and Ostade; the Netherlands had been overrun by French manners and fopperies, which threatened to destroy her independence and sap her spirit – or so it seemed to Van Effen; in a paper like the *Ware en Valsche Beschaving* (*True and False Politeness*) he ridicules the scented, powdered society of the day which knew no conversation except the exchange of fatuous, empty compliments, when even the independent Dutchman had become afraid to speak his mind lest he be condemned as a boor by the standards of Versailles.

Rather (he might have said) let us have the surly, respectless, hard-drinking democracy of former days. But not quite; there was a middle way between extremes; kindliness and good-nature were not wholly extinct nor were they the monopoly of any one class or nation. Then let each individual, each order of society and each nation be true to its own nature, without trying to give the peat-cutter the airs of the courtier or the Dutchman the graces of the Parisian dandy. To this extent it was the satirist's acid rather than the reformer's zeal that was called for, and two remedies were ready to hand – the practical philosophy of Locke and the wisdom of Addison – 'the English Socrates'. If Effen's wit is less effective than Addison's in his journal, it has other solid qualities of its own, and for all his close imitation of the English model, Van Effen manages to infuse something typically Dutch into his papers.

Van Effen helped to revive his countrymen's interest in the possibilities of their own language, largely by observing and following the examples of his English contemporaries – the bite and thrust of Swift, the easy simplicity of Addison, the colloquialism of Defoe – by using Dutch words where he could, and by avoiding Gallicisms. If contemporary Dutch prose was forced and stiff, that was not a fault inherent in the language but the short-comings of the writers' wit and imagination. Van Effen set out quite deliberately to eliminate those faults:

Since my aim is to bring entertainment and profit to all my fellow citizens, I will apply myself specially to considerations of intelligibility and perspicuity . . . Although I shall endeavour to flex my expressions to the matter, I will throughout strive to avail myself of the familiar style such as has been established by usage among people of birth and education . . . I will watch for long extended periods, in which it is the custom, after the Latin, to bring up the verb, upon which the whole sentence depends, at the end . . . Also I will, for the sake of clarity, carefully eschew those long parentheses . . . which in some of our writers, enclose and again enclose within themselves other parentheses like nest-boxes and necessarily produce confusion in the mind of the reader.[31]

Addison was Van Effen's hero and model, but he introduced many other authors to his readers – Shakespeare, Milton, Spenser, Swift (whose *Tale of a Tub* he translated), Sidney, Pope, Defoe (he translated *Robinson Crusoe*), Mandeville, Shaftesbury, as well as the philosophy of Locke, and the scientific writings of Newton. Van Effen did not, however, accept everything English with the indiscriminate enthusiasm which his opponents extended to everything French. He once described the English as 'one of the wisest and most reasonable Nations on the face of the earth' but he could be severely critical. The English press he condemned as irresponsible and licentious.

After the *Hollandsche Spectator*, the paper which did most to make English writing known in the Netherlands was the *Boekzaal* of William Sewell, a Dutchman of English descent, who carried on Van Effen's work of spreading English ideas in philosophy, theology and natural science. Once firmly planted, the love and appreciation of English literature did not die easily in the Netherlands. The novels of Laurence Sterne became tremendously popular. 'Sterne Clubs' became the rage. Literary Holland was submerged under a wave of anglomania. Dutch novelists were inspired by Sterne, Richardson, later by Scott and Dickens, as

Dutch poets were to be moved by Byron, Keats and Shelley.

The greatest strength of the culture of the Dutch Republic lay not in the literary but in the visual arts. Just as the early seekers after a Dutch literature in the 1570s had looked to France, to Ronsard and Du Bartas, so now the self-critical satirists of the riper bourgeois society looked to England for their models. Such Dutch prose and poetry as there was made little impact outside its native land where the Dutch language was virtually unknown. Yet, even so, the Dutch performed a cultural function as characteristic as their middleman role in world trade. They borrowed and they broadcast. The effects of the continuous diffusion of English ideas by Dutch writers, translators, printers and booksellers would be a worthwhile appendix to the history of the struggle for a free press in seventeenth and eighteenth-century England. It would show that in the age of the licensing acts and the libel laws – an age when English printing was technically and artistically at its worst – the presses of Amsterdam, Leyden and Utrecht offered a providential alternative medium of expression. When the parliament men controlled the licensing system they printed for the Royalists; when the office of Licenser of the Press was revived by Charles II they printed for the opposition.

In Holland the effects of this intercourse were not limited to the infusion into the Dutch vocabulary of hundreds of English words and phrases. In the eighteenth century, the packet sailing between London and Rotterdam or from Harwich to Helvoetsluys carried a steady flow of English books and newspapers to Holland. Stowed in with bales of broadcloth from Devon, and barrels of spices from the Indies, they passed on to France, Germany, Italy and to all Europe. Translations from Plantin and pocket-classics from Elzevirs found their way from Amsterdam and Leyden to Paris and Potsdam, Genoa, St Petersburg and London. It was part of the elusive process by which England was brought back into the main stream of the European tradition after the upheavals of the seventeenth century which threatened her with backward provincialism. Macaulay once wrote: 'France has been the interpreter between England and mankind'. That is to leave out the link which Dutch men of letters and Dutch printers formed between England and France. They gave France (and Europe) not merely the science of Newton and the philosophy of Locke but by a constant process of diffusion a whole range of the best in English literature.

9 A haven for philosophers

'Here is Antwerp itself changed into Amsterdam' – so wrote a new arrival from the Southern Netherlands in 1594. By 1685 a French visitor calculated that foreigners or descendants of foreigners with established homes in the province of Holland accounted for half the population. By far the largest (and wealthiest) group were Flemings or Walloons from the south. But they were far from being the only prominent newcomers. They were joined by Germans and Scandinavians, French, English, Scots, Jews, even by Armenians and Turks. The large towns were cosmopolitan to an extent unique in the seventeenth-century world. Universities like Leyden revived anew the old ideal of a community of scholars. English and Scots flocked to Leiden and Utrecht. In 1700 about a third of the students of Leiden were said to be British. Groningen admitted the best part of 3,000 foreign students in the course of the seventeenth century. At the end of the century the influx began all over again, as the Revolution of the Edict of Nantes sent thousands of Huguenots streaming across the border.

Almost all these foreign immigrants came in search of freedom from persecution, whether they were great merchants from Antwerp, skilled textile workers from Ypres or scholars from France or England. The independence of the town governments in the Republic and the absence of any central bureaucratic machine that could impose a tyranny of doctrine afforded a pretty safe insurance against persecution. The Dutch regents jealously guarded the right of asylum. The names of the depositors at the Bank of Amsterdam included a growing number of immigrants. But valuable though these economic attractions were, they meant less than the freedom of thought and conscience which the Republic offered. It was this which drew to Holland some of the boldest and most influential thinkers of the century. The most important were René Descartes, Baruch Spinoza and John Locke. Their thought was inextricably knotted together not only in agreement but in disagreement. But for the freedom and intellectual stimulus they enjoyed in the Republic, their work might never have seen the light of day, at any rate in anything like the form in which it became known to posterity.

Descartes was not a refugee from persecution in the ordinary sense. He was a French squire of independent means who shunned the chaos of the contemporary world (he fought in the Thirty Years War) and suffered from a restlessness that drove him from place to place until he found peace in the relative tranquillity of Holland. Here he set to work on philosophical problems and lived for the best part of thirty years. His most famous work the *Discours sur Methode* was printed and published in Leyden by Jean Le Maire. Most of his friends and acquaintances were drawn from the French-speaking Walloon community of Holland which had fled from Brabant. Although Descartes remained a professing Catholic, it was through his admirers among the Walloon Calvinists that Cartesianism was spread widely in Holland. It was characteristic, as Descartes himself noticed, that there was always a receptive audience amongst the Dutch for new ideas. In 1630 he remarked that almost all thinking Dutchmen were converted to the Copernican view of the universe.

Descartes thought and felt in a way typically French – detached, methodical, mathematical. Mathematics was for him attractive because it was logical, exact, orderly and (to the mathematician) self-evident. This was the key to truth. By such methods he tried to deduce knowledge from a starting point of doubt, in contrast to Bacon who tried to evolve general laws by induction from a mass of fact. Was there, asked Descartes, a truth which did not admit of doubt? Yes: it was formulated on his famous proposition 'Cogito, ergo sum'. (I think, therefore I exist.) The function of the mind itself proved that mind exists. From this he went on to deduce the existence of God, infinite, omnipotent, free and immortal. The

René Descartes, French by birth and education but mainly resident in Holland from the age of thirty-two, personified the combination of philosophical and mathematical method by which he pursued his quest for 'certainty'.

external world also existed outside God and Man. Its nature could be understood only in mathematical terms. This is not the place to try to analyse Descartes' philosophy. Undoubtedly, by emphasising the contrast between mind and matter he posed problems which he never satisfactorily solved, but (as Sir George Clark has said [28]) 'he set a problem and the setting of it was far more important than his failure to find a solution'.

Theologians were deeply suspicious of Descartes, some regarding him as a heretic or an atheist. Yet philosophers could never ignore him and his work is the starting point for much later thought. For Descartes brought a rational as well as an empirical intelligence to bear on problems long bogged down in conventionalism. By emphasising the centrality of the human mind he pointed the way to the individualism of later philosophers, not least of Locke himself. His 'psychophysics' on the other hand led to a more scientific view of the universe and his own mathematical enquiries themselves bore on astronomy and the working of its prime instrument, the lens.

Many of Descartes' followers extended and even exaggerated the rationalist element in his thinking. Baruch Spinoza was the greatest of his direct disciples who added breadth and humanity to the principles of Descartes. He was a member of the growing Sephardic Jewish community that lived round the Jodenbreestraat (Jewish Broad Street) near Amsterdam's waterfront. Its members were those *marranos* driven first from Spain to Portugal, then to Antwerp or Hamburg. From these and other temporary settlements these refugees from the Inquisition converged on Amsterdam, to whose life and culture they were to make a unique contribution down to the Second World War when large numbers of them were killed. It was not yet, in Spinoza's day, a wealthy or distinguished colony. Many of its members, including Spinoza, were poor. But there was already an air of the picturesque about the Jewish quarter which probably encouraged Rembrandt to live there. Rembrandt was in his mid twenties when Spinoza was born. At about the time when, in 1656, Spinoza was excommunicated for heresy with frightful curses from the Jewish community, Rembrandt was declared a bankrupt. But there is no clear evidence that they knew each other or even met. The possibility that Rembrandt's *Portrait of a Young Jewish Student* (in the Cleveland Museum) may be Spinoza is pure speculation. There is, alas, no portrait of Spinoza to compare with the superbly ironical portrait of Descartes by Frans Hals. The anonymous portrait nevertheless conveys something of the essential tranquillity, nobility, and humour of this remarkable personality.

Spinoza followed Descartes in many of his ideas, and like him used mathematical proofs of his propositions. But his work is intensified by a steady and consistent search for the unity of the universe as conceived in God. This makes it even more curious that Spinoza's name was frequently associated with atheism. Taken in conjunction with the long absence of translations into English or

The earliest known portrait of Nicolaus Benedictus de Spinoza (1632–77), painted by an unknown artist when Spinoza was aged about thirty-three. Herzog August Library, Wolfenbüttel.

HE WAS NO ATHEIST.

other European languages, the charge of atheism helped to prevent his true genius being appreciated for many years after his death. Possibly the known dislike of Locke was no help either. 'I am not so well read in Hobbes or Spinoza' wrote Locke in 1698, and added a few ironical remarks about 'those justly decried names'. Nevertheless he had evidently read (and been influenced by) both authors.

Spinoza wrote on many subjects – on pure philosophy, on the Old Testament, and on political theory. His ideal of the life of reason could only be realised in a moral community and through a social contract. In this later concept, as in many other respects, he was strongly influenced by Hobbes, but he diverged from Hobbes in one particular respect, and that respect was fundamental. As he himself put it, unlike Hobbes, he kept natural right intact. He therefore eliminated all obligation that was not based on self-interest. The subject obeyed his sovereign merely because it was to his own advantage to obey him. He suggested, in fact, that men are individualists, ruthless and uncompromising. Yet he was very far from suggesting that political or social chaos would necessarily result. The state was 'a union or agreement of minds', necessary for the genuine peace and freedom without which the life of reason was impossible.

His views as to how this should work out in theory and practice are set out at the end of his *Tractatus Theologico-Politicus* in a remarkable passage that combines earthy common sense with philosophic insight in a way characteristic of the man. If honesty, he says, is to be valued above servility, and sovereigns are to govern without submitting to mob rule, it is necessary to allow freedom of judgment and 'so to govern men that they can express different and conflicting opinions without ceasing to live in harmony'. In a democracy, the most natural condition of government, majority rule is necessary. But when freedom of judgment is limited, the worst evils follow. He quotes then the

city of Amsterdam, whose enjoyment of this freedom has made it great and admired by the whole world. In this flourishing state, this city without a peer, men of every race and sect live in the greatest harmony . . .[32]

This happy state of things had been interrupted by the disastrous dispute between Remonstrants and Counter-Remonstrants (orthodox and deviant Calvinists) earlier in the century. That crisis showed that laws passed to try and settle religious differences merely provoked men: they did not reform them. The real disturbers of the peace were those who attempted to abolish man's freedom of judgment.

Spinoza concludes therefore that it is impossible to deprive men of their freedom of judgment. This freedom will endanger neither the rights of the sovereign, nor the peace of the state. Not only will it not threaten piety; it is essential to the life of the state and community. Piety and religion consist wholly in the practice of charity and equity. Any other course of policy will be disastrous.

Good faith and honest dealing are undermined, lick-spittles and rascals encouraged, and opponents exult because concessions have been made to their anger and they have converted the sovereign to a creed of which they are the recognised interpreters.

He ends with a characteristic avowal of his own rational patriotism and a modest admission of his fallibility.

My treatise being now complete, it only remains to say expressly that it contains nothing that I would not willingly submit to the examination and judgement of my country's rulers. If anything I have written is in their judgement contrary to my country's laws or detrimental to the general welfare, I am ready to retract it. I know that, being human, I may have made many errors; but I have taken great pains to avoid error, and, above all, to see that everything I wrote should be in complete accord with my country's laws, with piety, and with sound morals.

In spite of these pious protestations the *Tractatus* was banned by the civil authorities in 1674 as seditious. That probably did not prevent its being widely read. Spinoza's other works were published posthumously. Whatever Locke may have said, Spinoza's ideas – his wisdom and tolerance especially – looked forward to the more liberal ideas of a later age and form in some respects a bridge between Hobbes and Locke himself. Difficult and labyrinthine as his argument often is, Spinoza had a gift of style in thinking – lucid, bland, yet shot through with arresting and even comic imagery – that prevents it ever being dull. 'For example' (he writes in the *Tractatus* discussing the relation between the power of the agent and the capacity of the object affected by that power) 'if I say I have the right to do whatever I wish with this table, I certainly do not mean I have a right to make this table eat grass.' In another place he discusses the distinction between truth and error, which he argues is a difference of degree. For example, he says, it can be illustrated by reversing sentences. 'My yard flew into my neighbour's hen.' All through his work runs the same thread. Philosophy was meant to help to solve the problem of how men should live.

Sir George Clark has summarised Spinoza's life and work as follows:

Although in a sense he eliminated the individual from the world, he favoured no ascetic self-denial, but taught, both in his books and in his own noble life, a reasonable virtue, for which the highest good was the intellectual love of God, a part of the infinite love of God Himself.[33]

He died comparatively young at the age of forty-four, having withstood the exile from his own Jewish community with characteristic stoicism. For many years he had eked out a living by grinding and polishing optical lenses. But this practical contribution to the age of observation may have hastened his early death from phthisis, through the absorption of glass particles into the lungs.

Neither Descartes nor Spinoza was in a direct sense a refugee. But Amsterdam provided for both the freedom they would not have found elsewhere in Europe. The third philosopher for whom Amsterdam provided a timely if temporary home was a direct victim of political upheaval. John Locke arrived in Holland in 1683. He was already a notable figure in England, but not yet primarily as a philosopher. He had gone to Oxford in 1652 when he was twenty, and remained a don until 1684 when he was ejected by James II. His entry to a wider world had come through Antony Ashley Cooper, later first Earl of Shaftesbury, upon whom he had performed an operation for a liver abscess which was not only spectacular but successful. He remained in Shaftesbury's entourage until the Earl died in exile in Holland in 1683. From Shaftesbury he acquired a vast range of practical political information. But he shared also the political penalty of being Shaftesbury's dependant.

We know that the last fifteen or so years before he was driven into Holland were the great formative years for Locke the philosopher. Most of his great works – on government, toleration and human understanding – were in an advanced state of preparation. Yet his five years in Holland were a vital phase in his development. When he arrived there in 1683 he was merely a refugee who knew not when or how he would ever return home. When he did return, in February 1689, he was a philosopher not only of high but unique reputation. He was valued because there was a practical, empirical edge to his thought that made men of the world respect him and ask his opinion. It can be argued that the change may well have come about from the enforced leisure of his exile. He had come away in a hurry, with few books or manuscripts. But Locke could carry most of what he needed in his head. The five years in Holland, so far from being wasted, were fruitful years of creative writing, pruning, polishing and editing. They helped to make him the Locke the world was soon to know.

He was fortunate to fall in with a group of thinkers, a number of them Huguenot refugees from France, others medical men – the preponderance reflects Locke's continuing interest in his original study – and ministers of the Arminian, latitudinarian persuasion. The Arminians had always been something of an intellectual *élite*, but, after the Synod of Dordrecht, an élite often under the shadow of bitter hatred from the orthodox Calvinists. Now, more liberal times had brought them back, especially at Amsterdam, and with their great learning they were enjoying a deserved intellectual and social prestige. Once again it was fashionable to be an Arminian. The acknowledged leader of the Arminians was Philip van Limborch, theologian and historian, who became a close friend of Locke. Through Van Limborch's circle of journalists and propagandists, Locke was to make his voice heard during his exile.

One of the most influential of Van Limborch's group was Jean le

BIBLIOTHEQUE
UNIVERSELLE
ET
HISTORIQUE
DE L'ANNE'E
M. D. C. LXXXVIII.
TOME ONZIE'ME.

A AMSTERDAM,
Chez WOLFGANG, WAESBERGE,
BOOM, & van SOMEREN.

M. D. C. LXXXIX.

The *Bibliothèque Universelle* was one of the many intellectual benefits gained by Holland from its enlightened welcome to Huguenot refugees after the revocation of the Edict of Nantes. Founded by Jean le Clerc, it printed many distinguished contributors, among them John Locke, then in hiding in Amsterdam.

Clerc who arrived in Amsterdam a year after Locke. Le Clerc was a powerful propagandist for Protestantism. The purpose of his *Bibliothèque Universelle* which ran from 1685 to 1697 was to mobilise Protestantism – openly in England, Switzerland and Holland, covertly in France – into an international force, a republic of letters. Amsterdam was the ideal centre. Nowhere else (as Le Clerc said) could he have carried on his propaganda so effectively 'because so many books are nowhere so easily published and sold as at Amsterdam.'

Le Clerc was introduced to Locke by Van Limborch. But Locke suffered from more than the normal academic shyness about publishing. It took a year to drag out of him his first article for the *Bibliothèque*: but once whetted, his appetite grew. He contributed numerous reviews, including one on Newton's *Principia*. In 1688, there appeared his most important contribution; an abridgement of the great *Essay* which was not to appear in full till after his return home. Long after the exile ended, Le Clerc continued to disseminate knowledge of Locke and his ideas. Other Huguenots helped too – Coste, Bayle and Desmaiseaux. But, as Dr Colie has said, it was Le Clerc who introduced Locke to the world and first jockeyed the reluctant author into print.

. . . in the city of Amsterdam where writing and printing were so natural to all good minds, Locke began to become Locke, and the obscure political exile turned into the philosopher *par excellence* of a new regime in thought.[34]

It is not the purpose of this brief survey to provide a detailed account of the thought of the three philosophers concerned. Rather to show how necessary, beneficial, perhaps indispensable, was the refuge and *milieu* which the Dutch Republic and its unique, if not perfect, freedom and tolerance provided for them. To show also how, perhaps not accidentally, they were related in their ideas. For though John Locke was an empiricist, interested in description as well as analysis, destined to found an English school of empirical philosophy, he also took his beginnings from Descartes. Unlike Descartes and Spinoza, Locke was no mathematician. Hence his divergence into the philosophic method he himself called 'plain historical'. Mathematical, rational, historical – Amsterdam was a broad bottom on which all could sit.

So could ideas that were less popular, even, in some eyes, far more dangerous. They came from England. Spinoza, as we have seen, was strongly influenced by Hobbes, the author of *Leviathan*, the propounder of ideas on sovereignty which to many good Dutch regents must have smelt of the pit. Yet unquestionably Hobbes made his mark on the Dutch. As Professor Kossmann has written:

One cannot open a scholarly political treatise, a doctor's thesis on law, a theological textbook, dating from the second half of the seventeenth century without seeing the author somewhere settling down to combat the *doctrina hobbesiana*. It seems to have been a matter of good manners.[35]

Yet the results were not always satisfactory. The critics seemed too often to discover too much merit in the bogey-man. Even upon the great Grotius, it was whispered, the beast had left its mark.

Tracing intellectual influences, like tracing aesthetic influences, is apt to lead the searcher into a quest for will-o'-the-wisps. There seems to be no doubt however of Hobbes's power, even in this republic of fragmented sovereignty where Leviathan was an anachronism. It would be pleasant to end by recording an equally specific Dutch debt to Locke. The year Locke returned to England, William van der Muelen, a young Dutch philosopher, published an elaborate defence of the Glorious Revolution. He hated absolutism, vindicated human rights and liberty and loved freedom. He was not merely a political commentator but a considerable theorist and philosopher, and his ideas bore a resemblance to Locke's which has been called astonishing. Alas for probabilities! Van der Muelen does not seem to have known Locke or his works. It is, however, plain that both writers were the product in part of a long interchange of philosophic and political ideas, part of a common climate of opinion formed not least in the relatively free air of the Dutch Republic.

10 Holland and Scotland

Trade was the link which bound Holland to many countries during the seventeenth century. There were few ports of any size in Europe where the trim, squat ships from Amsterdam and Rotterdam were not a familiar sight. But with Scotland the Dutch had special bonds. Scottish sheep from the southern uplands supplied a large part of the wool upon which the Netherlands cloth-making industry depended, and Middelburg and Veere had competed long and bitterly for the privilege of monopolising this lucrative trade. After years of wrangling and a score of indeterminate law-suits, the trade was eventually allocated to Veere on the island of Walcheren during the sixteenth century. There the Scottish staple flourished for two centuries, only dwindling into obscurity and decay when the Leyden cloth industry itself declined, finally disappearing with the revolutionary wars. At Veere the visitor can still see what the English traveller and essayist E. V. Lucas called 'the beautifully grave' *Schotsche Huis* on the quay, once the headquarters of the flourishing wool trade, and now a museum. This was the residence of the Scottish Conservators, the officials appointed by the king to govern the Staple. Amongst the seventeenth-century Conservators are two curious figures who deserve mention – Thomas Cunningham, who supplied the covenanting armies of the Scottish Parliamentarians with arms and munitions on Dutch credit, and Sir William Davidson – merchant, speculator, spy, amateur theologian and gun-runner – who followed Cunningham as Conservator from 1662 to 1671.

The ties which connected Scotland with Holland were not only commercial. In both countries Calvinism, with its emphasis on iron personal discipline and its rigid moral code for society, was the religion which appealed to men accustomed to extract a livelihood from a soil which grudged easy profits. To these men, religion and theology did not seem dry or sterile enquiries. Medieval man had seen the hand of God intervening in the most mundane affairs; the

Veere, the picturesque port on the island of Walcheren, was for long the centre of Scotland's trade to the Netherlands. The historic Scottish House survives today. It is a reminder of the important role which Scotland played as a supplier of wool for the extensive Netherlands cloth industry.

conviction persisted among Calvinists long after it had been weakened by the growth of rationalism in more comfortable societies. The Scottish passion for theological disputation was to become proverbial, but in the seventeenth century it paled beside an enthusiasm which pervaded the whole of Dutch society, of which a Jesuit remarked that everyone in the country from the chief rulers to the lowest yokel and sailor was thoroughly versed in the theology of Calvin.

Scottish religion and learning, which were strongly under French influence in the sixteenth century, fell under the spell of Holland in the next. While French Calvinism dwindled into sectarianism, Calvinism in Scotland and Holland rose militant and intolerant.

It would be difficult to overestimate the effect upon Scotland and upon Scottish religion of the Synod which sat at Dordrecht in 1619, or to exaggerate the veneration with which it was regarded by later generations of Scotsmen. Much to the satisfaction of the Scottish Calvinists the Synod of Dort condemned, the views of Arminius, and finally determined the shape of future orthodoxy in both Scotland and Holland. Henceforth, Arminianism in Scotland was to be identified with tyranny, illegal taxation, episcopacy, and even popery. To Scots, the Dutch Synod became known as 'the famous Synod of Dort', 'the renowned Synod', 'the venerable Synod'. Its conclusions were used as a basis and test of orthodoxy for three centuries. Books, theses, and sermons explaining and enlarging on its decisions were placed in the library at Glasgow College, and other Scottish university libraries can show similar collections of Dutch commentaries. The Westminster Assembly (1644–9), which determined religious standards for Scotland for later centuries, sat under its influence and inspiration.

The most famous Scottish divines of the seventeenth century – among them John Forbes, Robert Baillie, John Menzies, Samuel Rutherford – were strongly influenced by contemporary Dutch theologians both Predestinarian and Arminian, such as Voetius, Cocceijus, Hoornebeeck, Heinsius, Vossius, and even the great Grotius himself (though his religious views were a long way ahead of the bigotry of his age). John Forbes had himself been chaplain to the Company of Merchant Adventurers at Delft, and married a Dutch wife whom he took back to Aberdeen. Baillie had a cousin in Veere who sent him the latest Dutch theological works and kept him in touch with current discussions. Scottish theological works were often printed at Amsterdam, at this period the chief printing centre in Europe.

Meanwhile, the communities of Scottish traders and seamen in the principal Dutch cities and ports were settling down in an atmosphere which was politically and theologically congenial to them. At Amsterdam, the church of the Begyns, an ancient order of nuns, standing in a little court just off the Kalverstraat, was assigned to the Presbyterians in 1607. At Rotterdam, the States General and the magistrates gave permission in 1642 for a Scottish Church to be instituted and even provided funds. After two removals, the Scottish Church was finally settled at the south end of the Schiedam (or Scottish Dyke, so called from its being inhabited by large numbers of Scotsmen), by the Leuvehaven, used from time immemorial by Scottish shipping. Along with the Church went a Scottish school and poor houses. At Campveere, the first Protestant clergyman was appointed in 1587. At Delft too there was a wealthy and influential trading community: the sessional register of their church begins in 1645. Dordrecht, which became a regular Scottish staple port in 1668, supported a large Scottish population, and other communities were to be found at Flushing, Hertogenbosch, the Hague, Leyden, Middelburg and Utrecht.

These groups of Scotsmen in Holland made up a varied society, comprising all sorts and conditions of men from poor sailors and fishermen to the wealthy merchants of Rotterdam and the titled aristocracy at the Hague, from peaceloving pastors like the pious Robert Fleming of Rotterdam to the soldiers of the Scottish Brigade, who lived and fought as Scots for the House of Orange for more than two hundred years. This was the brigade which in 1578 sustained the brunt of the action at Reminant against the Spaniards, fighting 'without armour and in their shirts'. So much were they at home and so little interfered with that they were not naturalised until the American War. There was, at one time, at Zierikzee, a monument to a Henry Hume, an officer of the Brigade, described as a 'Captain in the service of the United Netherlands', who died at Delft on 28 May 1650. This curious English version claims to retain 'the spirit and quaintness of the Dutch original':

> When young I lost my Mother, but my loss I never knew;
> For oh! an aunt's maternal heart my final homage drew.
> In Sciences and arts, and tongues, and manners of mankind.
> As Captain of our infantry, as horse-lieutenant too,
> I shew'd unto my fatherland, a spirit bold and true.
> And after God for two full years had made our battles cease,
> He called me hence to spend with him the life of heavenly peace,
> I do not grieve, because I die and part with wealth and state,
> I only mourn, in that my aunt so sorely weeps my fate.

The ease with which these Scottish communities fitted into Dutch society contrasts strongly with the difficulties met with by most immigrant communities trading in foreign lands. There were no substantial differences between the systems of church government in the Dutch and Scottish churches. Many Dutch names appear amongst the deacons and elders of the Scottish churches in Holland, the ministers of which (though usually Scottish) were members of the Dutch *Klassikaal-Bestuur* or *Classis*. Relations with the Dutch ecclesiastical authorities were cordial, save for an occasional brush with garrison chaplains who were apparently inclined to 'conduct themselves in a violent manner'. Nor did the Dutch language hold any terrors for the Scottish settlers and their pastors, many of whom became well-known as preachers and theological writers in Dutch as well as their own language.

One consequence of these commercial ties and religious sympathies was that many Scotsmen went to the Netherlands for their university education. The process began with the pastors of the various Scottish trading communities and the chaplains to the Scottish troops serving in the Low Countries, who not infrequently attached themselves to the Dutch universities. It was sustained by the flow of exiles, English and Scottish, who sought refuge in Holland from the religious persecutions and political violence of seventeenth-century England and Scotland – men of such varied views and origin as John Robinson, pastor to the congregation of exiles at Leyden, the root from which the Pilgrim Fathers sprang, and Charles II himself.

To all this oddly assorted company, the universities of Leyden, Utrecht and Franeker offered refuge, hospitality and learning. The trickle became a stream, and hundreds of students, some English but mostly Scottish, studied at these universities in the seventeenth and eighteenth centuries. Over eighty matriculated at Leyden between 1620 and 1650. As we have seen, in 1700 one third of the students at Leyden were English or Scottish, and during the eighteenth century about 2,000 British students, a good proportion certainly Scots, matriculated there. Englishmen came there partly because of the lamentable state of the teaching at Oxford and Cambridge, partly because of the educational disabilities imposed upon English dissenters at the English universities. Scots were attracted to Holland partly, as we have seen, because Dutch theology was congenial to them, partly because of their unpopularity at Oxford (Boswell, himself educated at Utrecht, bears witness to this) and partly because Utrecht gave a training in

Roman law invaluable to a Scotsman. Utrecht therefore usually contained a contingent of young Scottish aristocrats studying (nominally, at any rate) law against the day when they should assume their estates. For to be a successful landlord in Scotland, it was at least desirable to be a tolerable lawyer. Amongst these were the second Earl of Marchmont and the third Earl of Argyll.

But of the generations of Scottish and English students who passed through the Dutch universities, from that ingenious Englishman, William Petty, who came back from Leyden skilled in mathematics, statistics, map-making and ship building, to the mercurial and Irish Goldsmith, and the errant, melancholy and Scottish Boswell, and of the imposing array of Dutch theologians, lawyers, mathematicians and scientists, at whose feet they sat, there is not room to tell here. Enough has been said to indicate the debt the two countries owe to each other. Remarkable affinities of outlook, temperament – even of language – drew Scots and Netherlanders together. The Scottish students at Franeker would not be alarmed by the Frisian shibboleth of 'bread, butter and green cheese': possibly their broad Doric was intelligible to the inn-keepers, landladies and tradesmen of the old Frisian town. Maybe it was Scottish students in Friesland who adapted that shibboleth into the Scottish rhyme:

> Bread, butter and green cheese
> Are good Scots and good Fries.

11 Dutch wars and Dutch pacifism

An empirical, largely self-interested and qualified pacifism was the theme of the merchant rulers of Holland. Apart from the arguments against war deployed by De la Court and De Witt, the wars themselves reveal most vividly the material interests that underlay those arguments and the threats to which they were exposed by war. Alone in Europe, the people of the Republic depended for their livelihood, necessities of life, and employment on a seaborne stream of goods that was the lifeblood of their economy. Much of their naval equipment came from the Baltic, that supplied the timber for their ships, the flax and hemp for clothes, canvas, sails, ropes, the iron for a hundred products in peace and war. Their herrings, a staple diet, came from the coasts of England and Scotland, salt from Biscay; their profits came from East Indian spice, Mediterranean silk and wine, English cloth. By the mid seventeenth century the Dutch economy had reached its peak, a brilliant demonstration of economic enterprise and ingenuity: but equally an economy that offered, in a world continuously at war, a thousand hostages to fortune. The nation that was in the most favourable position to strike at it was England; by 1652 she was poised to do so.

For three or four decades Anglo-Dutch relations had deteriorated. The English resented the economic superiority of the Dutch which seemed to bind them at every point. Policies designed to boost English industrial production and exports had cut little ice. In 1651 came the most ambitious and deliberate blow against the Dutch trade: the Navigation Acts which aimed to cut out the Dutch merchants and shipmasters from trade between England, her colonies and the rest of the world.

Not for the first time, conferences were called of both sides to try and reach agreement. But the forces of conflict were too strong. Even while the meetings were in session the Dutch were drafting instructions for Admiral Tromp. Significantly, the defence of trade

Through her world trade, Holland attracted a great influx of silver, much of which was minted and re-exported to pay for fresh foreign puchases.
Left to right: The golden ducat was used in eastern Europe; the silver state dollar in the Baltic; the silver lion dollar in the Levant trade; and the silver 'rijder' in the Far East.

was their first thought: the main Dutch fleet was to 'protect the waters in the track of the shipping for the Baltic and the North'. Another fleet was to escort home the East Indiamen and the rest to protect 'the great fishery which is of so great importance to the State . . .'. The dispositions were a fair indication of the maritime basis of the Dutch economy. They were exactly reflected by the instructions for the attack which the English were simultaneously preparing for Admiral Blake. His first task was to seize any Dutch East Indiamen he could find; to arrange that the 'Dutch fishery upon the coasts of Scotland and England . . . may be interrupted and disturbed and their busses . . . taken and secured'; finally, he was to attempt 'the disturbing and interrupting of the Dutch Eastland trade'. The correspondence of the two strategies was perfect. The Dutch problem was defence. The English opportunity was attack. The vulnerability of the entire system of Dutch trade was (like the vulnerability of British sea-borne trade in 1914 and 1939) an open invitation to an aggressor. And there can be little doubt that, in spite of Dutch provocation in the tropics, it was England that was in a mood of aggression in those years. Economically ambitious but frustrated, England was determined to achieve by force what she could not achieve by policy.

The immediate occasion of hostilities was a physical collision between the fleets of Blake and Tromp which met off Dover in May 1652. Tromp claimed he had lowered his topsails as a mark of courtesy and thought Blake should have been content with that. In the muddle that ensued, shots were exchanged and Tromp lost two ships. Dutch anger was rising. The Dutch commissioners in London decided that further parleying was a waste of time. In July the States General ordered Admiral Tromp into action. Pauw, the Grand Pensionary, wished him 'God's Blessing, Samson's Strength, David's Courage and Solomon's Wisdom!' But, as the war began, he reflected gloomily 'The English are about to attack a mountain of gold; we are about to attack a mountain of iron.'

The same thought occurred later (when the war was on) to a Plymouth sea captain who had captured a Dutch ship off the Dogger Bank. It was on its way from Sweden to Amsterdam. The English captain later recalled with some satisfaction his homily to his victim:

'I told him [said the captain] that the Lords States-General of Holland, being men of great abilities in state affairs, I did very much wonder that they should be so much overseen as to begin a war with the English, when (like

The Dutch attack on the Medway, 1667.
Oil painting by Jan Peeters, National
Maritime Museum, Greenwich.

an eagle's wings extended over her body) our coast surrounded theirs for a 120 leagues from Scilly to the Maas in Holland one way, and as many from the Orcades thither the other way; and the wind blowing above three-quarters of the year westerly on the coast of England, made all capelands and bays very good roads for ships to anchor at, so that converting our fisher boats into vessels of war, we could with them only readily and speedily put a stop to all our trade from France, Biscay, Portugal, Spain, the Mediterranean, Barbary etc., through the Channel to Holland, or force you to a circumnavigation round Ireland (as your east India ships) from all those places home, and having Ireland to clean ships at and victual, could easily intercept your trade that way also [36]

The homily was delivered 'over a bottle and pipe'. One can excuse a certain cockiness in the captor. The unlucky captive might well have answered that it was not the Dutch, who had everything to lose, who had started the fight, but the English. He might have added that his captor was simplifying and exaggerating the advantages of the English. Nevertheless, there was substantial truth in the English argument. The Dutch trade stood naked to attack. In the Channel, even the precious Silver Fleet that brought to Holland the Spanish treasure of Central America in payment for goods bought of Holland by Spain, had to run the gauntlet of the south-coast ports. It was under observation all the way from Plymouth to Dover. Yet the Channel could only be avoided if the Dutch ships from the south went north about around Ireland and Scotland; and that meant a serious increase in time, costs and risks.

English trade was very much less vulnerable. A Dutch squadron at the Thames mouth could wreak havoc, but the English economy was not exposed in the same way as the Dutch. Only the Newcastle-London colliers presented an open target, for coal was a necessity to Londoners.

The Dutch had one strategical advantage to set against a formidable list of disadvantages in war, but even this was a somewhat theoretical one. The prevailing winds being westerly, it was a dangerous business for an English fleet to try to blockade or invade the Dutch coast, consisting as it did of shallows and sandbanks. Conversely it was easier for a Dutch fleet to raid or blockade the English coast, as the Second Dutch War was to prove. But nobody supposed that the risk of any Dutch military force of importance being landed in England was serious.

If the Dutch were at a disadvantage strategically, they were no better placed administratively. They had more warships and probably more experienced seamen. But their ships were smaller and their firepower was less. The officers, mostly merchant navy men by training, brought the independence of their old trade with them. They did not take easily to the discipline vital to a fighting navy. Moreover the organisation to which they were subject was itself far from coherent. The five Admiralties which wielded authority reflected the same cumbrous decentralised government as the constitution itself. Tromp, as lieutenant-admiral, exercised a control over a federated navy that was even more ill-defined than the political or military power of the Stadholder.

This would have been less serious if the task of the Dutch fleet had itself been easier to define and execute. But here came the most serious problem of all. The basic task, as it appeared to the merchants and regents, was to defend Dutch trade, shipping and property on the high seas from destruction. Hence it seemed reasonable to the merchants that the Dutch fleet should be disposed so as to afford maximum convoy protection along the sea lanes, especially through the Narrow Seas and to the Baltic. Their conception of sea power was essentially defensive. Not so the admirals'. Tromp and his successors were all dedicated to the same theory of sea power as essentially offensive. To restrict the fleet to convoy duty alone was to disperse its destructive power and fritter away resources that alone could bring total victory instead of mere survival. The first task of the Dutch navy should therefore be to seek out the English enemy and destroy him in pitched battle. The best defence lay in attack. By seizing the initiative, the threatening weapon could be struck out of England's hand before it could be used. This, argued the professional sailors, was the most economical and effective way to use their most formidable weapon – their knowledge of sea and ships. But time and again it proved too risky a theory to find favour with the regents and the merchant community. And, indeed, though theoretically sound, there were serious difficulties in putting it into practice. Weather, and the contingencies of battle always seemed to ensure that victory always fell a long way short of what victory ought to mean.

The first example of this was not slow to materialise. Blake managed only to scatter the fishing fleets off Scotland but missed the main prize – the returning East Indiamen. The 'mountain of gold' was not, after all, such easy pickings. Tromp, out to smash the English fleet in a decisive engagement, missed both squadrons (Ayscue and Blake). After that, the demands of trade protection began to pile up. The main problem was the famous 'Silver Fleet', carrying fifteen or sixteen million guilders, which was expected to make for Amsterdam up the Channel in August. Admiral Michael de Ruyter was appointed vice-commodore in charge of a new fleet to clear the Channel for this convoy. For the threatened disruption of Dutch trade had impressed on the authorities how vitally interconnected were all these different branches of Holland's world network. The silver won by trade from Spain and her colonies was necessary to pay for spices from the East and naval stores from the Baltic – areas of a normal payment deficit. If herrings from Scotland and salt from Biscay disappeared, the Dutch would be unable to buy corn from Danzig. And so on. The fabric of Dutch trade was a unity. By the autumn trade congestion was serious. Four hundred merchantmen were waiting to sail for Holland, the Mediterranean and Indies. All required convoy.

As winter came, the Dutch strategic dilemma was put bluntly to the States General by Tromp. 'I could wish to be so fortunate,' he wrote, 'as to have only one of the two duties – to seek out the enemy or to give convoy; for to do both is attended by great difficulties.' Harassed, but stout-hearted as ever, he nevertheless attacked and defeated Blake off Dungeness a few days later. When he attacked again in March in the Channel, he had the worse of the fight. But by a stupendous feat of seamanship he managed to escape round Cap Gris-Nez with the remainder of his fleet and a large convoy.

Nothing could now disguise the fact that the English had won control of the seas. So far as trade was concerned the Dutch could only take avoiding action, routing their valuable ships round the north of Scotland and hoping for the best. Tromp succeeded in persuading the States General that to convoy on a general scale was beyond his resources. The most hopeful policy was to restrict trade, keep as many merchant ships in harbour as possible, and thus release the fighting ships for the hope of successful onslaught on the English. But at the Gabbard, fifty miles east of Harwich, Tromp was smothered by the heavier firepower of the enemy. He limped back behind the Dutch sandbanks. The great blockade of Holland had begun in earnest.

The effects were quickly felt. Corn prices at Amsterdam rocketed, herrings disappeared, public morale slumped. 'Tis pitiful here,' said a letter from Holland in June 1653 'to see the amazement amongst all sorts of people; yea, the merchant never looked with such a countenance, which is sad to see upon the Exchange.' By August, banks were breaking, East India shares tumbled, starvation and riots were the talk of the land. Even the Grand Pensionary, De Witt, imperturbable as ever, had to admit that the fatherland stood in 'a great troubled and desperate state.' A brave attempt to break through the Blockade by Tromp failed in August and Tromp himself was killed.

Fortunately for Holland, the arrival of Cromwell in supreme power in England coincided with the growing realisation by the English navy that to maintain the blockade indefinitely put English morale also to a severe test. Cooped up in ships permanently at anchor the English officers and crews became increasingly irritable and mutinous. The peace of the following year therefore came as almost as much of a relief to the English as to the Dutch. And in pursuance of his policy of a great Protestant alliance, the Protector was content with magnanimous terms. The war had nevertheless revealed the crucial weaknesses of a Dutch economy which had evolved in terms of economic efficiency, peace, and business as usual. It was not designed to cope with the presence of a determined aggressor. Commanding a ring of ports from Harwich to Plymouth, the English had shown themselves capable of blocking all the most vital arteries of Dutch trade.

The First Dutch War had a lasting effect on opinion in Holland and England. It confirmed the English in a belief in their own strength, and the sovereign merits of trying another smack against the Dutch. Cromwell's decision to wind up a successful war seemed to many of the jingoists premature and ill-judged. Meanwhile, Dutch opinion became all the more cautious about international involvements that might lead back to the disasters of 1653–4. It was not long however before another ugly mood of belligerency brought Anglo-Dutch tensions to a head once more. But this time the results were to be surprising.

Cromwellian idealism and prudence, judiciously combined, kept tension down until the Restoration. It welled up again in 1660, but so long as Clarendon held the reins as principal adviser to Charles II the forces of conflict were kept in check. With De Witt on the

Overleaf: The start of the Second Anglo-Dutch War in 1664 was   195
preceded by a curious outburst of anti-Dutch propaganda
in England. Some of this took the form of common abuse
in rhyme for consumption by the London mob, whose violence,
fanned in this way, might force Parliament into a war
desired only by a minority. British Museum, London.

other side, likewise dedicated to a workaday sort of peace, he even
brought about a treaty of agreement in 1662. Yet all the mutual
congratulations that accompanied the occasion could not disguise
the ugly fact that the wound was stemmed, not healed. Behind and
before the scenes, intrigue and dissension went on. The disputes
that had provoked the first Anglo-Dutch war were largely domestic
or at any rate European. Now they spread, until, without exaggeration, they could be described as world-wide. In the East Indies, in
North and South America, in the West Indies, on the coast of
West Africa, one dispute after another arose to aggravate the
troubles in Europe. The flames were fanned by a curious alliance
of bellicose interests at the English court. It included members of the
court, mostly Catholic followers of the Duke of York, ambitious
young naval officers like the wild Robert Holmes (much distrusted
as a trouble-maker by Samuel Pepys) and a group of City merchants
who recollected the brave days of the first Dutch war and re-
gretted that it had been so untimely concluded.

By 1664 it was plain that the war party were winning. Clarendon
was no longer the power behind the throne. Sober, sensible men
like William Coventry and Pepys could do little to stem the anti-
Dutch tide. Every weapon of propaganda was dragged up and put
to good use. One pamphlet (designed for more or less thoughtful
opinion) asked: 'But if it should come to a Warre, is this the proper
juncture of time for it?'. 'Leave that (says the pundit) to the exact
wisdom of our superiors, who, as they are higher, see further than
we.' But the conclusion was not in doubt. '. . . never was anything
so unanimously applauded by men of all persuasions and interests
as a *Dutch Warre*.' 'What we want' the Duke of Albemarle said
bluntly 'is more of the Trade the Dutch now have.' Other pamphlets appealed to cruder tastes. (*The Dutch Boare or A Description
of Hoggland*, illustrated overleaf, is a fair example.) Against this
background of propaganda the war opened.

A *Dutch man* is a Lusty, Fat, two Legged Cheese-Worm :
ter, Drinking fat Drink, and Sliding, that all the VVorld knows him for a
a *Low-lander* ; for he loves to be down in the Dirt, and *Boar*-like, to walk

THe *Dutch* at first,
  When at the worst,
The *English* did relieve them :
  They now for thanks,
  Have play'd base Pranks
With *Englishmen* to grieve them.
A   Those Spider-Imps,
  As big as Shrimps,
Doe lively Represent,
  How that the States
  Spin out their Fates
Out of their Bowels vent.
B   The *Indian* Ratt
  That runs in at
The Mouth of Crocodile ,
  Eates his way through,
  And shews well how
All Nations they beguile.
C   The Monstrous Pig,
  With Vipers Big,
That Seven-headed Beast,
  Shews how they still,
  Pay good with ill
To th' *English* and the Rest.
  The Vipers come
  Forth of the Wombe,
With death of their ownMother:
  Such are that Nation ,
  A Generation,
That rise by fall of Other.
D   One of the Rout
  Was Whipt about
Our Streets for telling lyes :
  More of that Nation
  Serv'd in such Fashion
Might be for Forgeries.
E   Their Compass is
  An *Holland* Cheese,
To steer a Cup of Ale-by :
  The Knife points forth
  Unto the North
The Needle these Worms sail-by.

: a Description of

N D.

ture, that is so addicted to Eating But-
llow. An *Hollander* is not an *High-lander*, but

F   Their Quagmire Isle
     ('Twould make one smile)
In Form lyes like a Custard :
     A Land of Bogs
     To breed up Hogs,
Good Pork with *English* Mustard.
G   If any asks,
     What mean the Casks ?
'Tis Brandy, that is here :
     And Pickle-Herring,
     (Without all Erring :)
'Tis neither Ale nor Beere.
H   Those Two you see,
     That yonder bee
Upon the Bog-Land Walking ;
     Are Man and Wife ,
     At wofull Strife
About last Night's work talking.
     He Drinks too long ;
     Shee gives him Tongue,
In Sharp, hot-scolding Pickle,
     With Oyle so glib
     The same for Tib,
Her tipling man to Tickle.
     I Spin all Day,
     You Drink away
More then I get by Wheeling :
     I doe'lly part ,
     Sayes he, Sweet Heart ,
For I doe come home Reeling.
I   The *Holland* Boare,
     Hath Stock-Fish store,
As good as can be eaten :
     And such they are,
     As is their Fare,
Scarce good till soundly beaten
K   Their State-House such is,
     It stands on Crutches,
Or Stilts, like some old Creeple
L   Frogs in great Number
     Their Land doth Cumber,
And such-like Croaking People

Unmasked.

No nation stood to gain more than the English from Waghenaer, the Dutch cartographer. Ironically, this map of the Thames estuary charts the very approaches navigated by the Dutch ships in their celebrated attack on the English navy in the Medway in June 1667. This was the blackest hour in a war when everything had gone wrong for England. Sheerness fort was captured. Among the ships towed away was the pride of the English fleet, the *Royal Charles* (see pages 188–9).

The real crisis came in April 1664, when 'great numbers of merchants' of the City of London presented a petition to the House of Commons. Their complaints were not novel. The Dutch (they said) had obstructed their foreign trade, incited natives to oppose them, destroyed their warehouses, proclaimed themselves 'Lords of the Southern Seas' and generally behaved with intolerable arrogance. The Commons showed themselves suitably sympathetic, agreeing to pray His Majesty 'to take some speedy and effective means' to redress 'the wrongs, dishonours and indignities done to His Majesty by the subjects of the United Provinces . . .'. Matters did not move quite as swiftly as the war party hoped, but steadily they were wearing down the King's reluctance. He still hoped that England could get what it wanted without war. Yet by the end of 1664 it was clear that the continuous scuffles at sea were degenerating into a real war. The Commons voted Charles two and a half million pounds for a war. Yet as Pepys reported, the earlier mood of reckless optimism was swiftly diminished. Reflecting men were already wondering whether the Dutch War was, after all, going to be the walk-over the warmongers expected.

The first bad omens came when the London Turkey merchants, a rich and powerful City group, were told flatly by the Admiralty there were not enough ships to send out a convoy for their trade. The two sides were reckoned to have fleets of roughly equal size, but the Dutch had evidently learnt a lesson from the first war. Their new ships were now heavier and stronger, with 'greater timber and irons being putt into them'. They had longer keels and more brass cannon. Nothing like this new fleet had ever been seen in history (so the intelligence went) – 'very great ships, and well man'd and gun'd, full of great animositie and earnestness to fight'. Public morale in Holland was equally high. The Dutch did not want a war, but if it came they were ready to fight to the death.

Conversely, English morale was not so good. Not for the first

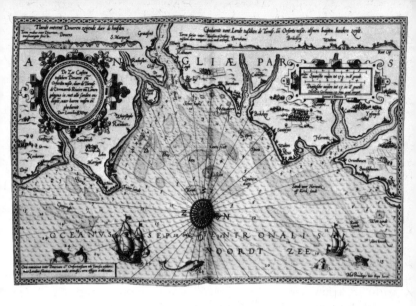

time, nor the last, the high command thought that their job was to fight the previous war over again, or perhaps more accurately to begin again where Cromwell had left off. James, Duke of York, the lord admiral, accordingly appeared off the Texel in April with a hundred or more sail to blockade the Dutch trade. Yet, somehow, nothing went according to plan. The organisation of the fleet was poor, victualling inefficient. There were signs of mutiny. Volunteer officers, bored by sitting at anchor with nothing to do, began to think (as Clarendon wrote with some satisfaction) that 'the war was not so necessary as they had thought it to be'. The end was that the blockade had to be lifted, the Dutch came out and there was an indecisive action off Lowestoft in June. But the unreal calm was at last broken. Action followed swiftly. The Dutch East Indies fleet got home after taking shelter in Bergen; more important, so did De Ruyter, with a rich convoy of merchant ships. The Duke of York, the lord admiral, retired from active command and the opprobrium of failing to capture the rich prize at Bergen fell on his successor, the Earl of Sandwich. When Pepys walked through the holds of the single large Dutch ship that was captured he was overcome by an ecstasy of chagrin to think what Sandwich had missed.

The greatest wealth . . . in confusion that a man can see in the world. Pepper scattered through every chink. You trod upon it, and on cloves and nutmegs I walked above the knees, whole rooms full. And silk in bales, and boxes of copper plate . . .[37]

Meanwhile, affairs in general were going from bad to worse. London was in the grip of the plague. The navy only had half the money it needed to meet its commitments. One after another the Continental powers hastened to join the enemy. 'The Dutch War goes very ill . . .' wrote Pepys as the year ended. When the war came to life again in the spring of 1666 it was to present England with the fiasco of the Four Days Battle, first hailed in London with bonfires and victory dances, later with mourning as the truth dawned that it was a hopeless defeat. Thereafter the war fell to pieces. The Great Fire in September made matters worse. Londoners spent a cheerless winter, with the Dutch harassing the coal supplies from Newcastle. Contrariwise, Dutch morale had soared even higher with the certain knowledge that the English were in real difficulties. 'The Dutch' remarked a naval officer friend of Pepys, 'do fight in very good order and we in none at all.'

These were the conditions in which it was decided to limit English naval strategy for 1667 to what was politely described as 'a flying fleet'. This was really a confession that a genuine strategy was no longer possible. The bulk of the fleet would have to be laid up. A few cruisers would attempt raids on enemy convoys. Such a policy could 'preserve for a year longer, but the end of it must be ruin' (as Pepys observed). It was humiliating to see the lord admiral, instead of being at sea, going from port to port supervising the defences – 'a sad consideration and shameful to the Nation especially for so many proud vaunts as we have against the Dutch . . .'.

By February the English were virtually sueing for peace. When their terms proved too ambitious, the Dutch improved the shining hour by what was to be perhaps the proudest exploit in their naval history. Sailing up the Medway they captured and towed away the giant battleship, the *Royal Charles*. They landed at Sheerness and were rumoured to be at Dover and down the whole coast as far as Dartmouth. 'By God' wrote the harassed Pepys 'I think the Devil shits Dutchmen.' The news was exaggerated and the raids of no fundamental military importance other than that of lowering England's naval strength more than ever. But the blow to English pride was unsupportable. Cock-a-hoop, the Dutch were able to make a very satisfactory peace.

There was still another Anglo-Dutch war to follow in 1672, but there was to be little reality in it. The peace of 1667 was really the turning point in Anglo-Dutch relations. For once again the climate of opinion was changing. Many in England who had lent support to an anti-Dutch policy between 1650 and 1667 were now beginning to doubt whether wars between Protestants were not after all a dangerous diversion of effort. For an increasing body of opinion, the new menace – comparable to the former threat by Spain – was of a French Catholic hegemony in Europe. In any event, the wars had been disappointing. It had become evident that for the time being at any rate the old efficiency of Commonwealth days had disappeared from English military and naval affairs. Even the first war had shown both sides that truly decisive actions were rarely possible in these naval encounters. The death at a crucial moment of a brilliant commander could wreck the chances of real victory. So could a change of wind, a bad storm, a fog or a heavy mist. Time and again a battered fleet was able to slip away under cover of darkness, evading all attempts at capture, ready to emerge again in a matter of days or weeks and rejoin the fight. Naval warfare was an expensive and maddeningly frustrating business.

Holland's enemies in England were apt to dismiss Dutch pacifism as hypocrisy. 'It is *mare liberum* on the British seas but *mare clausum* on the coast of Africa and the Indian Seas.' So wrote Sir George Downing, a malignant enemy of the Dutch. There was a measure of truth in the argument. Yet neither side paid any great attention to the colonial scuffles that were always breaking out in one or another part of the world. England also seized New Amsterdam without putting the Dutch to war as a result. The Dutch attachment to peace was genuine precisely because it sprang from a genuine material stake in peace. Apart from the losses of ships, cargoes, and seamen, occasioned by the wars, there were other, political and social, risks. Even the naval wars emphasised the social divisions of the Republic. When bread and herrings were scarce, the people rioted. Mob rule threatened the cautious, well-ordered oligarchic system of government. Even more dangerous to social order and tranquility was a land war such as that which the French inaugurated in 1672.

The Second Anglo-Dutch War (1664–7) has been aptly described as 'a war of tradesmen'. The French attack on Holland five years later also had a strong economic motivation. The nationalist economics of Colbert had precipitated the tariff of 1667 which hit the Dutch harder than any other nation. Like the English Navigation Acts, it was intended to eliminate the intrusive Dutch middlemen from the French trading system. For Colbert the amount of world trade was fixed. Each nation had to fight for its share. In 1670 Colbert wrote: 'Commerce is a perpetual and peaceable war of wit and energy among all nations'. France had 'conquered' every rival except the Dutch. But the new great French trading companies were 'like armies', attacking the Dutch everywhere as 'mortal enemies' and would soon wear them down.

French mercantilism was becoming markedly less pacific by 1672. Colbert prepared an elaborate plan to take over the entire

Dutch trading system and put it under French control. Far from being the pacific victim of his aggressive royal master, Colbert was a man of his time who fully supported every military move to destroy the Dutch economy. His economic pressure contributed not a little to the outbreak of war in 1672.

In June 1672 the French crossed the Rhine. By July they were in Utrecht, in the heart of the Republic. If the French had been able to march straight on their goal, that would have been the end. But the usual professional military caution about by-passing fortified towns held up the advance long enough to allow the famous 'water line' defences to be put into operation. A wide strip of flooded land running from the Zuiderzee to the river Lek separated the French army from the demoralised Dutch troops. The flooding was not accomplished without serious resistance from the local farmers. Some towns also opposed the flooding – Gouda in particular saw no merit in this kind of heroic suicide. To the losses of the floods was added the grim work of building fortifications and field works. All these discontents rebounded on the heads of the regents and the States party. It was not difficult for the Orangists to whip up resentment against the De Witts and the so-called 'Loevestein faction' who could ingeniously be shown to be the cause of all the trouble. Twenty years in power do not usually leave a government popular. Now all the popular underlying support for the House of Orange welled up into a movement for the restoration of young William as Stadholder. The regents were to be ousted.

1672 was known – according to political preference – as the Year of Miracles, the Year of Murder, or the Year of the Press. The 'miracle' was the salvation of the Republic, for it saw the French advance first stemmed, then reversed. The 'murder' was the murder of the De Witts. The 'press' was the flood of pamphlets mostly attacking the States regime and demanding every kind of reform from a simple return of the House of Orange to a variety of political experiments of a more or less democratic kind. Many of them involved a theory of contract between government and people that recall for an English reader the heady democratic visions of the Commonwealth or herald the Lockeian theories of the 1680s.

In the end the Republic was to have none of them. In Holland as in England, class affinities were not easily broken. Faced with the realities of power, the Prince of Orange showed no inclination to risk an alliance with radical idealists or democrats. Among the regents were many Vicars of Bray ready to desert the De Witts and join the winning side. Everywhere the upper classes in town and country were sufficiently alarmed by the threat of mob rule to close their ranks. Orangists began to see that the French (and some of the English) were no more friendly to an Orange regime than to a Loevestein regime.

So the melodrama faded. William of Orange, displaying the courage as well as the diplomatic skill for which he was to become famous, carried the day. Oligarchy continued. Democracy retreated. Social continuity was achieved. The old gang remained in power at the cost of sacrificing a few victims. The pattern of events was not unfamiliar. The realism of the Dutch had once more been demonstrated and a national synthesis of Orangists and Oligarchs was in sight. French hopes of a take-over of the entire Dutch economy were thwarted. The Treaty of Nijmegen that ended the war in 1678 revoked the tariff of 1664. As an economic crusade to liberate France from Dutch economic control, the war of 1672–8 failed as signally as the English war of 1664–7 had also failed. But in the Republic itself there was only a modified satisfaction. Once again it had taken a war to frighten the ruling classes of the Republic into a full realisation of their danger. The danger came from without and within. Many in both parties had thought that Holland commanded loyalties in France and England. They were now disillusioned. Others saw how precariously the social order was perched on a diminutive base of military or police power.

The lessons of the 1670s – that war was disastrous for the Republic – could not be applied to the full. This was a century of war. The Republic could not contract out of it. But steadily the Dutch defined more accurately and narrowly those ultimate objectives of national policy which were worth a war. And they were few: to keep the French out of the southern Netherlands; to preserve their economic interests in peace and to extract the utmost advantages from neutrality in war. These were the residual criteria of national policy after all extravagances had been purged away. Distrust of war as a weapon of policy was not a form of idealism or of cynicism with the Dutch, it was born of realistic understanding of the politics of seventeenth- and eighteenth-century Europe. No student of history who fails to grasp this can hope to understand the belief in neutrality that was to last until 1939.

12 A trading empire

Between the truce with Spain of 1609 and the Treaty of Breda with England in 1667, the Dutch created a new colonial trading empire. They did it in competition with two other powers – a declining Portugal, upon whose colonial heels they trod nearly everywhere except in North America, and the English who were also preparing themselves for colonial adventure. Few spectacles in modern history are more remarkable than the explosive expansion of Holland and Zeeland, these two small waterlogged provinces that formed the heart of the Republic. For more than a century the Netherlands economy had been developing on the principle of a division of labour. The Netherlanders concentrated on those trades and industries that yielded high rates of return. The less profitable they left to others. They therefore naturally extended their enterprise to these remote areas of the world that were confidently expected to yield, if not gold and silver, at any rate spices, fine textiles, tobacco, sugar and similar products of high scarcity value. They were already equipped by experience to navigate in far waters. There was probably no better school of navigation and seamanship than the seas between the Bay of Biscay and the Baltic.

The chosen instruments of colonial expansion were the East India Company and – much later and less successful – the West India Company. Like the government of the Republic itself, like the navy too, these companies were organised on a more or less federal basis. The East India Company, granted its charter in 1602, was the result of a belated realisation that the original pioneer companies were all getting in each other's way and that as a result profits were lower and costs higher than they could have been. But the new corporation, ruled by its seventeen directors (the *Heeren* xvii), retained six regional 'chambers' based on the old companies at Amsterdam, Middelburg, Delft, Rotterdam, Hoorn and Enkhuizen. The corporation disposed of the talents of Dutch navigators who had formerly served with the Portuguese. Nor had the earlier voyages, ill-organised though they were, been entirely wasted. Cornelis Houtman's first voyage of 1595 had been literally a 'pilot plant' for later expeditions. The Amsterdam merchants who organised it had aquired all the information they could about the journeys of Drake and Cavendish. Where possible they had employed pilots and sailors who had served in earlier English expeditions. (Among those on board were John Davis and James Lancaster, who were later to be in charge of the English East India Company's expedition to the same waters.)

The same pattern of control as had manifested itself in the politics of the Republic was now repeated in the East India Company. Gradually the small 'chambers' fell under the dominance of Amsterdam. By the end of the century a group of a hundred or so Amsterdammers held nearly half the capital of the Zeeland chamber. More than half the total capital of the entire company was held in Amsterdam. In the second half of the seventeenth century, the nature of this Amsterdam control itself altered. Active merchants played a diminishing part. Regents – rentiers, professional administrators – came to dominate its affairs.

The West India Company presented a strong contrast to the older company. It was the brain child of the Calvinist, Orangist party, strongly influenced by southern immigrants whose driving ambition was to strike a last fatal blow at Spain and Portugal. Oldenbarneveldt had delayed its foundations in the interests of his policy of conciliation with Spain. Once he was out of the way, the West India Company went forward. Amsterdam was less enthusiastic about this enterprise than it had been twenty years earlier about the old. Even so it subscribed on a very large scale. By 1670 half the capital of the West India Company was likewise owned by Amsterdam shareholders.

Yet there the resemblance between the companies ended. In the East the Dutch company forged ahead. By the mid-century, it had

established itself by conquest in the Moluccas, at Batavia; Malaya, at Pulicat in India and Zeelandia in Formosa. It had made monopoly contracts with native rulers like the Sultan of Ternate. Elsewhere it traded alongside the English or Portuguese in competition for the favours of the local chieftains. This last was to be, in spite of additional conquests after 1650, the most important area of trade. In everything except the spices of the Moluccas and Ceylon, that is to say, the Company's business was highly competitive. Hence the presence of those who, from the formidable founder of Batavia, Jan Pieterszoon Coen, onwards, believed in a policy of conquest to eliminate European competition and bring local rulers under control.

Coen had laid down his formula to the directors in 1614 and it was in very clear terms:

Your Honours should know by experience that trade in Asia must be driven and maintained under the protection and favour of Your Honours' own weapons, and that the weapons must be paid for by the profits from the trade; so that we cannot carry on trade without war nor war without trade.[38]

This was strong medicine for the cautious *Heeren* at Amsterdam.

The West India Company was founded largely on the initiative of stoutly Calvinist merchants of South Netherlandish origin. But its combined mission of trade and Protestantism against Spain and Portugal in Brazil and elsewhere was not successful. It lost its New Netherland colony to the English and its West African posts gradually dwindled. Compared to the East India Company, it was a failure.

Fortunately perhaps for them, there was never much they could do about it. As a much later official at Batavia remarked, 'The Directors in the fatherland decide matters as it seems best to them there; but we do here what seems best and most advisable to us.'

Territorial conquest nevertheless remained limited – in Asia to Java, the Moluccas and Ceylon, in South Africa to the Cape settlement. Originally founded to trade in pepper and spices, the Company changed tack later in the seventeenth century. As European demand for oriental textiles grew, the importance of spices declined. In the next century textiles were joined by tea, coffee and porcelain as homeward cargoes. Within its area of conquest, the Dutch Company, like its English rival, became a territorial colonial power in the eighteenth century. Yet even here it remained, as Professor Boxer has said, 'an alien body on the fringe of Asian society'. The trading activities of the Dutch did little to alter the fundamental forces of economic, social or religious custom which decided the shape and structure of society in Java or Ceylon. *A fortiori* the same was true of areas like the Indian mainland, China and Japan where the Europeans came as traders not as conquerors.

The Cape of Good Hope was incidental to the Company's plans. Soon after their foundation they had tried to seize Mozambique as a port of call for their ships to be re-victualled. They failed. In 1620 the English East India Company had taken formal possession of the Cape, but then failed to occupy it. It therefore remained until Jan van Riebeeck took it in the name of the Dutch Company in 1652.

The Cape was not a safe roadstead for shipping (in fact it was very dangerous) but it provided a healthy stopping place, and reduced the appalling mortality at sea that marked these long voyages to and from the East. But as a settlement it was, in the eyes of the directors, an incubus. Its main function was to supply victuals for the Company's ships. The main duty of the governor was to keep the costs of food and maintenance as low as possible. The

On the Coromandel and Malabar coasts of the Indian mainland, the Dutch
replaced the Portuguese until in turn they were squeezed out by British
and French. Surat especially (*above*) was a leading trading centre.
Philip Baldeus was a rigidly orthodox Calvinist pastor, dedicated to
white supremacy, who worked in India and wrote a description of
Malabar and Ceylon (1672) from which these pictures are taken.

second half of the century therefore saw a conflict between the
Company and the 'free-burgher' colonists who had been allowed to
farm the land and provide provisions. They wanted, not unnaturally, to get the best prices they could for their produce. As
long as the Company rule lasted, the conflict went on. 'Trekking',
a phenomenon often thought of as a nineteenth-century peculiarity,
began in the late seventeenth century. It was the instinctive reaction
of men trying to escape from the rigid autocracy of Company rule.
Visitors already noticed the difference between the urbane bureau-
crats, professional men and merchants who formed the Cape
community itself, and the rougher, tougher *boeren* who had moved
out further and further into the hinterland. It was a distinction
which was to last to the present day.

The West India Company was from the start a belligerent
mixture of trade and religion. Most of its directors were strong
Calvinists from the south whose dominating idea was to combine
business with a religious crusade against popery. They were almost
uniformly unsuccessful. After a promising beginning, the campaign against Brazil became hopelessly bogged down, its costs an
endless drain on the finances of the Company. Sugar, the commodity
in which the Company in Brazil principally dealt, was a highly
fluctuating and speculative business. Markets were impossible to
predict, profits precarious. The brilliant capture of the silver fleet
by the Dutch Admiral Piet Heyn in 1628 enabled the Company to
declare a bumper dividend but it was almost the last for thirty-five
years. The West African trade yielded some profit too, but this was
absorbed in the enormous costs of the fiasco in Brazil. The Company ended by going into the slave trade, especially the profitable
but illegal export of slaves to the Spanish American colonies. Yet as
a whole the history of the West India Company was a dreary tale
of muddle and near-bankruptcy. It showed how wise was the normal Dutch policy of keeping politics and religion out of business.

Mallagam

Kerck-huys   Kerck

Originally discovered by Henry Hudson, an Englishman employed by the Dutch West India Company, New Amsterdam was the centre of the Dutch trade and settlement on the American east coast for over half a century, until it was captured by Captain Nicholls in 1664. The English changed its name to New York, but Dutch place-names, family names and even craftsmanship (e.g. silverware) have survived to the present.

Like the East India Company, the West India Company never penetrated the tropical countries to which it traded. Like the older Company it established one colony of white settlement – New Netherland on the banks of the Hudson and the shores of Manhatten Island. In 1609, two years after Christopher Newport had brought his battered ships into Chesapeake Bay and initiated the English settlement of America, Henry Hudson sailed west in search of a north-west passage to India. Hudson, though English, was in the employment of the Dutch East India Company. He failed to find what he was looking for, but found instead the river which bears his name. This he believed to be the opening of a channel which would lead him through into the Pacific. When this optimistic assumption proved wrong, his backers lost interest. But that was not the end of the story. Other merchants had spotted the possibilities of the fur trade. A company was founded. Blockhouses flying the Dutch flag sprang up, one on the island of Manhatten, another – 'Orange' – where Albany now is. The trickle of immigrants began to realise that New Netherland had other commercial possibilities too. Surrounded by the more populous and growing settlements of New England and Virginia, the Dutch colony was strategically placed to act as an entrepôt for the entire east coast.

Unfortunately, the directors of the West India Company at home, under whose aegis the colony stood, failed to see eye to eye with the colonists. A dispute arose not unlike that which was to arise between the Cape colonists and the directors of the East India Company. The directors hedged and vacillated over schemes of further colonisation. The governor was at loggerheads with the colonists over their demands for more say in local affairs. By 1649 three delegates of the citizens of the colony embarked for home to submit petitions against the entire system of control by the West India Company. The leading spirit was Adriaan van der Donck, a man of remarkable and articulate vision. His petition on behalf of

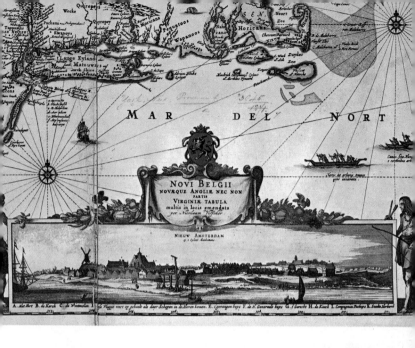

the languishing colony ended with a plea for more immigration, more civic freedom. Only this, he said prophetically, could save the existence of the colony:

The most terrible ruin will follow and this province will become the defenceless prey of its neighbours. The Dutch free burghers already living there will be forced to seek refuge elsewhere or to subject themselves to a foreign nation. The very name of New Netherlands will be lost and no Dutchman will any longer have any say in affairs here.[39]

The mission was not altogether without effect. The reins were loosened a little. A modest measure of self-government was allowed. Immigrants flowed in (many of them foreigners) but the colony remained small. Meanwhile, from 1660 onwards, the English government was set upon enforcing a re-invigorated navigation system designed to prevent the Dutch from buying from or selling to English colonies except in carefully selected areas of trade. The Dutch colony in North America cut clean across these ambitions. Its most profitable business was in smuggling goods through to New England and buying (so it was said) wool from the New Englanders to supply to the Dutch cloth industry in defiance of all the regulations which were trying to restrict that supply. An economic challenge of this kind from a militarily weak and isolated foreign community was too much to be tolerated. After a suitably pious prelude of protest and claims based on heavily doctored history, an expedition set out to capture the colony. In 1664 New Amsterdam became New York. There was no bloodshed. (A common Protestantism counted for something, even in the seventeenth century.) But another chapter of Dutch colonisation and settlement was at an end, though Dutch continued to be spoken amongst the descendants of the settlers for another century. But Dutch craftsmanship continued identifiably in such manufactures as silverwork. Personal ties remained strong. Late in the eighteenth century a gigantic land speculation in Pennsylvania and New York was floated by a Dutch company, the *Hollandsche Land Compagnie*. It was an American of Dutch descent who cut the Erie Canal and poured the first kegful of lake water into the Atlantic. It was the first of the famous members of the Roosevelt family, Nicolas, who organised the first steamboat service from Pittsburgh to New Orleans. The Dutch did not quickly forget their traditional skills.

In the meantime, other Dutch discoveries had taken place which were to have consequences equally great to the British Empire. These were the opening up of the south-west Pacific. There was a tradition that south of New Guinea lay a great continent – a tradition which possibly originated in half-remembered tales of earlier voyagers, possibly in the old theory that the southern hemisphere must contain as much land as the northern in order to maintain the stability of the earth – a nice instance of how the Middle Ages occasionally came to the right conclusion for the wrong reason. 1606 saw the first authenticated discovery of Australia by the Dutchman Willem Janszoon who, coming from Bantam in the *Duifken*, crossed the dangerous region of shoals and islands separating New Guinea from Australia and penetrated into the Gulf of Carpentaria, reaching the west coast of Queensland. The Dutch explorers were not impressed by what they found in these lands of promise; they wrote:

This extensive country, for the greatest part desert, but in some places inhabited by wild, cruel, black savages, by whom some of the crew were murdered; for which reason they could not learn anything of the land or waters, as had been desired of them, and, by want of provisions and other necessaries, they were obliged to leave the discovery unfinished; the furthest point of the land was called in their Map, Cape Keer-Weer (Cape Turn-Again) [40].

Ten years later, the Dutch accidentally discovered western Australia. A Dutch ship taking the route south of the tropics from the Cape of Good Hope to Java overran the passage westwards before turning north to Java and sighted the west coast of Australia. During the following decade, the whole of the west coast was charted, and in 1627 another Dutch ship explored about half the southern coast. The new continent was christened *New Holland*, but thereafter Dutch interest flagged; Janszoon's successors conceived no more affection for it than he. It promised no spices, food or even fresh water. Meanwhile other Dutch seamen were exploring in the north and in 1623, one had crossed the Gulf of Carpentaria and discovered Arnhem Land.

Dutch enterprise in the south-west Pacific culminated in the voyages of the great commander and navigator Abel Tasman and his chief pilot and planner, Frans Visscher, sailing under the patronage of the governor-general of the East Indies, Antony van Diemen. The immediate motive of the expedition was strategic; in South America the Dutch were at grips with the Spaniards; their

problem was to find access to the Spanish colonies in South America without having to go all the way round the north Pacific and down the Californian coast, risking the twin hazards of calms and adverse winds. Tasman's aim was to steer a passage south of Australia; his voyage brought him to an island (Tasmania) which he named Van Diemen land; then, turning east into the open ocean, he came to an unknown land which he called New Zealand. He followed the coastline to its most northerly point which he called after his patron's wife, Maria van Diemen, then, convinced that the west wind track to South America was navigable, he sailed back to Batavia by the northern coast of New Guinea.

Tasman's discoveries made him the greatest explorer since Magellan; they were not to be surpassed in importance until the time of Cook. As a result of his voyages and those of his predecessors, the Dutch had come to know a great deal about western and northern Australia, though they still mistakenly believed New

By the early seventeenth century, Dutch explorers had reached the ends of the world at both poles. Evidence of this enterprise is (*left*) a page from the journal of Abel Tasman (*c.* 1603–59), recording an encounter with natives during his Australasian voyage 1642–4; and (*right*) a pair of compasses, left in a cache by the Nova Zembla expedition of 1596 and discovered there by Carlsen almost three centuries later (see page 117).

Guinea to be contiguous with north-east Australia. They also knew the southern coast as far east as Tasmania. But these were not the most attractive or fertile stretches of the south coast and the east coast – the regions which make up the greater part of the populated continent today – remained outside the scope of their knowledge and interest. Obsessed by the narrow conception of colonial trade as a quest for spices, the Dutch explorers were blind to the vast potentialities of these continents which they discovered, charted and left sprinkled with Dutch names which have survived to this day.

For sixty years after Tasman's great voyage, interest in New Holland and New Zealand languished, to be revived at the end of the century by a reformed English buccaneer, William Dampier. Another half century was to pass, however, before England produced the greatest of all the South Sea explorers, Captain James Cook, a sailor by profession, a brilliant cartographer and a man of powerful intellect and sterling character, under whose influence the south-west Pacific finally became a sphere of British development.

To summarise: within half a century of their earliest voyages, Dutch traders and adventurers had sketched the future course of European colonial development. They had laid the foundation of an eastern and a western Empire; they had established a settlement in the pleasant lands of south Africa and another on the Atlantic seaboard of America: they had discovered and charted considerable stretches of territory in Australia and New Zealand. Yet the Hollanders' enterprise failed to live up to its early promise. Except for the East Indies and some islands and territories in the West Indies and South America, the Dutch settlements either stagnated, or fell supinely before the aggressive enterprise of newcomers, or simply failed to take root.

The sequence of events in Dutch colonial developments underline the genius and the limitations of this remarkable people – bold exploration, efficient commercial exploitation, followed by a withering of enterprise and growth. Why did this happen? One fundamental trouble was diagnosed by Snouk Hurgronje, a great nineteenth-century Islamic scholar. He characterises the history of the Dutch East India Company in the East in these terms:

The first act of the Netherlands-Indian tragedy is called 'Company', and it begins almost exactly with the 17th century. The chief actors deserve our admiration for their indomitable energy, but the objective for which they worked, and the means they employed to attain it, were of such a kind that we, even with the full application of the rule that we must judge their deeds and doings by the standard of their times, have difficulty in restraining our aversion. The 'experiment' began in such wise, that the inhabitants of Asia came into contact with the dregs of the Dutch nation, who treated them with almost unbearable contempt, and whose task it was to devote all their efforts to the enrichment of a group of shareholders in the Fatherland. The servants of this chartered Company, kept all too short by their employers but not less greedy for gain than they, displayed a picture of corruption which overshadows the worst of what the Oriental peoples are accused of in this respect.[41]

This can be accepted, or rejected, as an orthodox statement of liberal anticolonialism in general. It cannot be proved that the Dutch were any better, or any worse, in their attitude to the peoples with whom they came into contact through colonial exploration and trade than the Spanish, Portuguese or English. The lump of commercialism was certainly leavened by the presence of some remarkable men whose vision went far beyond the narrow limits of their day. The charge of 'corruption' does not go to the root of the matter either. It is at least doubtful whether the Dutch were in general more 'corrupt' than the other European traders and administrators overseas. At home, the Dutch merchant had a reputation for honesty in business dealings. While those who went to the tropics were unlikely to be the best representatives of their kind, 'corruption' is a doubtful answer to our question. Indeed the question itself needs to be divided into two: why did the white settlements either disappear or fail to develop? What went wrong with the tropical colonies?

As regards the settlements at New Netherland and the Cape, the trouble lay with the form of organisation and government that was adopted, and the failure of the original concept – the 'trading' concept – to adapt itself to any broader image of development. The sequence of ideas and hopes for New Netherland has been outlined earlier. So have the conflicts between the citizens, the West India Company and its local governor. The concept was plainly restrictive. In spite of a relatively liberal attitude in religious affairs urged upon the governor by the Company at home, there was little civic freedom and only a slender degree of self-government. The colony's fall was admittedly a matter of *force majeure*. Maybe it was doomed anyway. An earlier more imaginative

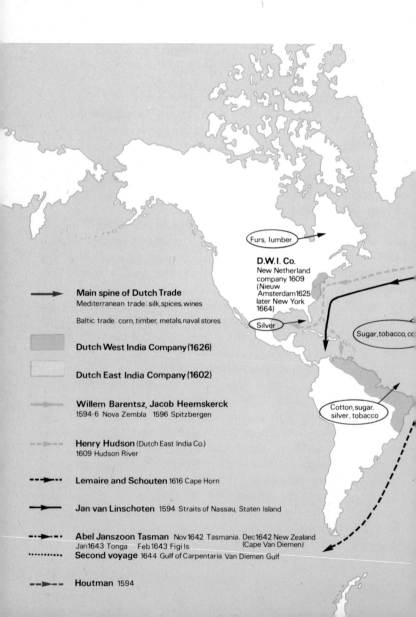

World map of Dutch trade
routes and voyages of discovery;
the dates are of landfalls
or other Dutch claims.

Furs, lumber

D.W.I. Co.
New Netherland
company 1609
(Nieuw
Amsterdam 1625
later New York
1664)

Silver

Sugar, tobacco, co

Cotton, sugar,
silver, tobacco

→ **Main spine of Dutch Trade**
Mediterranean trade : silk, spices, wines

Baltic trade : corn, timber, metals, naval stores

Dutch West India Company (1626)

Dutch East India Company (1602)

➤ **Willem Barentsz, Jacob Heemskerck**
1594-6 Nova Zembla 1596 Spitzbergen

⟶➤ **Henry Hudson** (Dutch East India Co.)
1609 Hudson River

--➤-- **Lemaire and Schouten** 1616 Cape Horn

⟶➤ **Jan van Linschoten** 1594 Straits of Nassau, Staten Island

··➤·· **Abel Janszoon Tasman** Nov 1642 Tasmania. Dec 1642 New Zealand
Jan 1643 Tonga   Feb 1643 Figi Is. (Cape Van Diemen)
········ **Second voyage** 1644 Gulf of Carpentaria Van Diemen Gulf

--➤-- **Houtman** 1594

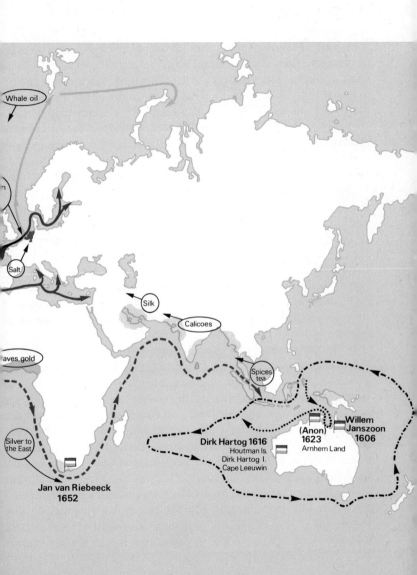

Whale oil

Salt

Silk

Calicoes

aves,gold

Spices tea

Silver to the East

Jan van Riebeeck 1652

Dirk Hartog 1616
Houtman Is.
Dirk Hartog I.
Cape Leeuwin

(Anon) 1623
Arnhem Land

Willem Janszoon 1606

Dirk Gerrit 1599

and more generous policy on immigration might have created a stronger, more confident and more powerful colony, but it is at least doubtful. Here the very size of Holland was a major factor.

By comparison with England, even more with France, the Republic was small. It was also relatively tolerant, comfortable and prosperous: not a country to create immigrants so much as to receive them. Here as at the Cape the flow of immigrants later was to include a higher proportion of Huguenots and Germans. At the Cape as in America, the rule of the Company – the East India Company in this case – was restrictive and oppressive. The Company saw the colony simply as an appendage to its navigational and commercial organisation. The colonists existed for the sake of the Company, to victual its ships and provide a stopping-place for health and recreation. The duty of the Company was to keep the colony as small as possible, and as light a charge on the Company's budget as could possibly be arranged. Even late in the eighteenth century its numbers were barely above the ten thousand that were estimated to live in New Amsterdam at the time of its capture in 1663.

It would be absurd to expect contemporaries to have foreseen the whole complex course of future history that was to make these policies seem so narrow and shortsighted. What can fairly be said is that many of the colonists themselves protested against the restrictive outlook of both great companies. A man like Van der Donck at New Netherland pleaded eloquently for more freedom, economic and civic, and there can be little doubt that he was influenced by what he saw in the neighbouring societies of English settlement to the north and south. This was not so much intelligent design on the part of the English as a lesser degree of commercial efficiency. The entire English effort in North America was steadily to take on a greater aspect of individual freedom and enterprise as Company organisation fell into desuetude. It was the very perseverance of the Dutch, the concern for detailed commercial organisation, that prevented the devoted servants of the Dutch Companies from seeing that what was needed in the longer term was not more organisation but more freedom.

The story in the tropical possessions was quite different. The collapse of the West India Company can be explained in terms of bad objectives, bad management and bad luck. After the loss of Brazil and New Amsterdam, all that was left was a handful of small settlements in and around the Caribbean. In the East, however, the possessions of the East India Company survived, trade became more diversified, surviving into the Napoleonic Wars and of course until the Second World War and later. In 1939 Netherlands India was a model of colonial administration. It is easy now to point out weaknesses. The fact that so many men who went East were less than desirable meant that such women as could be induced to accompany them were no improvement on their consorts. The Dutch free burghers could only marry with the consent of the local Company boss, and they could only marry Asian or Eurasian women who had been baptised into Christianity and whose children could be baptised as Christians.

The influence of Calvinism, such as it was, in these areas of tropical trade and company organisation, was almost entirely negative. Pastors willing to undertake missionary duties were very few. But the few who did volunteer spent too much time fighting local manifestations of popery (in the former Portuguese possessions) or unorthodox forms of Dissent (as in New Netherland and the Cape Colony). Religion did nothing therefore to modify the general statement made earlier that the Dutch remained culturally on the fringe of these Asiatic societies (unlike e.g. the Portuguese in Brazil where a complex interaction of religion and culture took place). Certainly in the Islamic regions, the failure of Calvinism to adapt itself in any way to local social or cultural

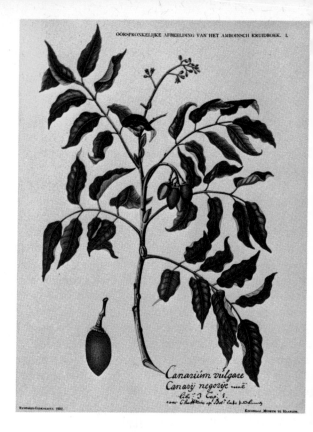

Canarium vulgare
Canary negorij ...

conditions served to strengthen Islam, and thus in the end to weaken the foundations of Dutch power.

Admittedly it is not altogether fair to blame the Company or the Calvinist Church for what happened. The Company did its best to provide pastors; far more than its English equivalent. But the conditions it laid down were onerous and unrewarding. The pastors were at the beck and call of the Company. Little incentive to emigrate! Once again, the truth seems to have been not that too little thought and organisation was provided but too much. It was idealism and vision that was lacking.

Not that it was lacking altogether. When it came it was sometimes from an unexpected quarter. It was the great admiral Piet

The spirit of observation and inquiry was common to all talents, whether scientifically or artistically directed. Thus (*left*) Rumphius, working for half a century in Amboyna in the Moluccas, brought his exquisite reproductions of fauna and flora to the level of artistry despite their botanical purpose; while Rembrandt's careful drawing of a shell (*below*) shows his affinities with the more practical observation of his contemporaries in science.

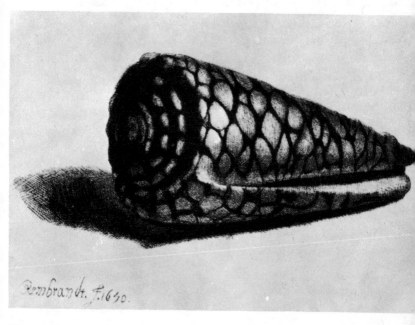

Heyn who explained why the Indians felt such hatred for the Europeans. It was the Indian who was wronged. Was it surprising he should turn on his torturer? That was no reason to retaliate.

... if we treat the Indians savagely and harshly we will give them cause to hate us. And that hate will quickly strike deep roots and turn their hearts away from us ... Let us make sure we do not offend God through any unfair dealings, and instead of serving Him as a rod for others [the Spanish and Portuguese] incite Him to lay a rod on our own backs.[42]

Headquarters, well-meaning as usual, were constantly issuing instructions to their local agents to treat native chieftains, leaders, merchants and populations fairly, justly and decently. Force might

Three pictures from the later seventeenth century which illustrate the sweep of Dutch economic power in the eastern seas: (*left top*) Mauritius (captured from the Portuguese in 1598 and named after Prince Maurice of Nassau); (*left bottom*) Hughli, in Bengal; (*right*) Amboyna (Larike) in the Moluccas.

be necessary as a last resort, but should never be resorted to lightly. This was all very well. When at the receiving end there was someone of the strong-arm school of thought like J.P.Coen, the conclusion was in no great doubt. But even in Coen's entourage there were those, like Laurens Reael, who disagreed emphatically and courageously with Coen's policies of force and subjection. Even as early as 1618, Reael, a man of great cultivation and a member of the Muiden circle, was expounding the economics of what an economist would describe as the backward-sloping curve. The Company, he said, were deliberately bringing such small supplies of food and necessities into the Moluccas that all incentive to the natives to gather the clove crop had disappeared. It paid them better to cultivate food for themselves. '. . . we are so narrowly grasping over our profits and earnings that we do not allow anybody to earn a farthing or a penny from us.' Reael continually urged more liberal policies towards the native populations at large.

Nor did the colonial *élites* lack scientists and scholars as well as liberal reformers. Rumphius, 'the blind seer of Amboyna', worked for half a century at Amboyna in the Moluccas until his death in

1702. He spent a great part of his life collecting and illustrating material on the fauna and flora of the islands. His work on the geology and palaeontology of the islands is still valuable. What Rumphius did for the Moluccas the Baron van Rheede tot Draken-stein did for the west coast of India. In Brazil the governor-general subsidised similar work on the botany, geography and meteorology of the region. In Surinam, a learned lady, Maria Sybilla Merian, produced a fine work on entomology. Others, like Daniel Havart, De Jager and Kaempfer were at work on the history and ancient languages of Persia, Java, Ceylon, and Japan.

The life, work and ideas of such men must be allowed to modify the impression that Dutch colonial endeavour in the seventeenth century was an unrelieved pursuit of profit by a hard-fisted organisa-tion made up of what Hurgronje called the dregs of society. This can easily be shown to be a romantic exaggeration. The truth is less spectacular and less melodramatic, but it is not less explana-tory. The original aim and purpose of the Companies was trade, and trade it remained. There is no need to doubt the intention of the directors to have a proper regard to the welfare of their servants, even of the natives. But their first duty was to their shareholders. With regard to the rest, their responsibilities were legally secondary to their responsibilities to their shareholders and to the Company itself. Morally, they were limited by prevailing ideas (common to many outside the circle of commerce) of the superiority of Europeans to non-Europeans, of Christians to non-Christians, of Protestants to Papists, and of Calvinists to other forms of Dissent. Within the matrix of Company organisation they put these ideas into execution with a dutiful eye to minutest detail and a fidelity to principle that was often as remarkable as that characteristic of servants of great public corporations of the twentieth century. In the end, this fidelity to duty was probably more disastrous than all the corruption, gross and petty, all the private trading, smuggling and jobbery that seemed to contemporaries (and has often seemed to latter-day liberals) to be the root of all subsequent evil. A looser organisation, a less formal dedication to detail might have allowed an easier transition from a commercial to a socio-political basis of relationships. More freedom, less bureaucracy might have opened up paths to the future that were closed to eyes riveted on commercial and financial detail.

There was another, even more impalpable factor. The history of the Republic from its inception had been one of a precarious balance between the forces of civilised, self-interested tolerance and tight-lipped theocracy. They had struggled for mastery at home. By and large the forces of tolerance and freedom had won. But by a narrow margin. The loving precision that went into a perfect lens or a flower painting or a *grisaille* could turn into the theological pedantry of a Voetius, conducting with opponents battles over the *minutiae* of usury that lasted for decades. Of the latitudinarianism that saved the Republic from this pedantry and kept it in the paths of Erasmus, of Grotius and of the more liberal traditions of the regents, too little proved to be exportable. The Republic had been fused in a crucible of freedom. The ideas of freedom spilled over into the age of discovery and enterprise. Then they were ossified into legal regulations for the conduct of trade, executed with precision by a conscientious bureaucracy. The age of overseas expansion ground to a halt not least through an assiduous attention to commercial detail.

13 Decline

The Dutch Republic did not collapse. Its golden age simply faded and withered. Vulnerable to war, its economic life from time to time had showed signs of strain during the wars with England and France in the second half of the seventeenth century. Yet the underlying strength of the economy was such that it was able to weather successive storms and emerge into the eighteenth century still wealthy and powerful. Dramatic disaster was postponed until the French revolutionary wars. Nevertheless, a slow change was steadily eroding the foundations of the Republic and making any further true growth difficult if not impossible.

Down to the French Revolution, the volume of Dutch international trade remained about the same, ventures in international loans and credits even increased, so did agriculture; but industry declined perceptibly and there was little if any increase of population. While other nations, England especially, were going forward, Holland remained virtually where she had stood since 1648. Alongside this economic stagnation, historians have discerned a stagnation of spirit, a sapping of creative power, an end of greatness and a slide into social artificiality.

Economic 'decline' was associated with the passing of the conditions which had enabled the Dutch to achieve their unique position in the seventeenth century. The relatively rapid increase of population in the sixteenth century had created gaps in Europe between areas that produced more food than they needed (the Baltic in particular) and those (like Spain and intermittently England) which were short of food. The ports and towns of Holland, Amsterdam especially, had rapidly become a central entrepôt where European supply was adjusted to demand, not only in respect of food but of commodities and products of every kind, including a growing stream of colonial goods.

This broking function was a precarious one. Some of the economies supplied by the Dutch, like those of Spain, Italy and

Scandinavia, continued to be backward. Here and there the Dutch middleman and shipper was still needed. But, after 1660 especially, other European nations began to move forward perceptibly. The population explosion in Europe ended. England and France both entered an age of ambitious economic planning, aiming at self-sufficiency and industrial expansion. In England Royalists, Parliamentarians and Cromwellians might disagree on everything else; they were unanimous in their desire to restrict and hamper Dutch trade and navigation, and they put it into action by a series of navigation acts. These limited the volume of cargoes the Dutch were able to carry to England and virtually excluded them from trade with her colonies. The abundance of Dutch pictures and Dutch tiles and bricks that found their way to England in the eighteenth century may be partially explained by the import restrictions placed on other Dutch cargoes that originated in countries other than Holland. France raised tariffs against Dutch imports in 1664 and 1667. Both countries clapped on protective tariffs to help their own infant industries. Subsidies and bounties were offered to English agriculture and industry. Steadily, such skills as textile dyeing and printing, glass making, paper making, sugar refining, linen bleaching and scores of other industries were coaxed into life in England and France. Even shipbuilding, in which the Dutch had been so long supreme, was making headway. 'Pinks' built at Whitby and Scarborough incorporated many of the best features of the flyboat. It was no longer necessary for the English to buy their merchant ships in Dutch ports.

On every side the Dutch faced growing competition in trade and industry. The textile industries of Leyden reached their peak output and profits in the 1660s. After that they began to level off as the 'new draperies' of East Anglia and the serge industry of Devon steadily made headway in English and overseas markets alike. French textiles offered increasing competition in France itself and in

Mediterranean markets. Here was irony indeed: the new industries the Dutch had helped to generate in England and France now proved serious rivals to Dutch traders and manufacturers who for a brief spell had had the markets to themselves.

Another force besides competition was at work to obstruct further economic growth in Holland. Foreign visitors to Holland from the mid seventeenth century onwards were struck by its very high level of indirect taxation. Sir George Downing, English agent in the Hague to successive Cromwellian and Stuart governments, a venomous hater of the Dutch but a shrewd economic observer, wrote home in 1659:

. . . it is strange to see with what readyness this people doe consent to extraordinary taxes, although their ordinary taxes be yett as great as they were duringe the warr with Spaine, and indeed such as would make any man admire at, a barrel of ordinary beere payings 40 stivers excise, and 5 stivers for bringinge in, each stiver beinge more than an English penny, and every man payes the 6 penney of the rack rent of his landes, besides an infinity of other taxes, so that I have reckoned a man cannot eate a dishe of meate in an ordinary (inn) but that one way or another he shall pay 19 excises out of it. This is not more strange than true.[43]

A French traveller Étienne Pavillon wrote in 1680 in his *Stances sur un Voyage en Hollande*:

The State is so encumbered with debts, its subjects so loaded with imposts, salt-taxes, and traitors, that the wise foreigner surely has every right to be astonished that the former pays out annually what it owes and the latter manage to discharge their obligations.

These burdens on the people's food meant demands for higher wages. Higher wages meant higher costs for manufacturers, higher prices for customers, difficulties in selling to export markets. In 1657 a writer claimed that the English cloth industry only paid half what the Dutch had to pay in wages because of the high cost of houses and victuals in Holland which dictated the high rate of wages. Seamen's and dockers' wages, indeed all wages connected with trade as well as manufacturing industry, were affected in the same way. By the end of the seventeenth century Dutch wages were between ten and twenty per cent higher than English wages.

Gregory King, the social statistician, summarised neatly the comparative situations between Holland, England and France in a calculation of 1696. Gross average income per head in Holland was the highest in the world, but so was taxation – almost all derived from indirect taxes on necessities like bread, meat, salt, beer, fish, butter, paper, etc. The result was that the man-in-the-street had less left over for consumption than in England or France. With a population less than half that of England or one sixth that of France, Holland was raising a public revenue larger than that of England. The average Dutchman was paying nearly three times as much in taxes as his equivalent in England or France.

Why this onerous burden of taxes? Briefly, the costs of defence.

Try as they might to avoid war in Europe, to construct a rational, profitable economy, the Dutch could not insulate themselves against the power politics of Europe. Ineluctably the Dutch economic miracle was to be overtaken by the iron logic of fact.

Writing in 1782, a Dutch statesman, Van de Spiegel, set out dispassionately the situation of the Republic. For well over a century the debt of the Republic had grown and with it the burden of taxes. The cost of war had steadily increased. Ships, weapons, equipment, all cost more. Each war was fought not only at the charge of the current generation but of posterity. War had become a luxury the Republic could no longer afford in a world where great and richer neighbours were growing every day bigger and richer but where Holland remained the same size.

Another eighteenth-century Dutch writer, Luzac, pursued the

social consequences of Holland's dilemma. The heavy burden of taxation (he wrote) resulted in the flight of skilled workpeople – a kind of eighteenth-century brain drain. Parents refused to put children into jobs where there was no money. Parishes were nervous of too many marriages that might put up the poor rates. Men preferred prostitutes to wives. Skilled crafts were thus starved of recruits, while indifference, indolence and sloth characterised the lower orders.

For one reason or another, the social scene was becoming steadily more gloomy. Every European country in the eighteenth century had its own melancholy record of unemployment, under-employment, poverty and mendicancy. England, soon to move most rapidly into revolutionary economic change, was no exception. Even mechanical invention and powered industries did not necessarily remove the large pockets of misery and poverty that afflicted the poor of all ages. But in Holland the social problems of poverty and unemployment seemed to defy all the efforts of philanthropy and paralysed the nerves of economic enterprise.

Such conditions suggest that a society can reach a state where all enterprise simply becomes numbed and helpless. High taxes and costs operating through relatively high wages and perhaps anti-quated gild and craft organisation bore a considerable measure of responsibility. Industries that employed large capital in the shape of buildings, plant or machinery (e.g. sugar refining or brewing) survived better than those which incurred large labour costs (e.g. textiles).

The irony of the situation is clear.

The Dutch had sought and won independence from Spain (and others who sought to replace Spain as overlord of the Netherlands) precisely because they saw the fateful logic of dynasticism. Dynasticism meant the blind pursuit of dynastic ambition. That meant war. War meant expense. Expense meant taxation. Taxation meant the strangling of trade. An uneasy combination of feudal conservatism, Calvinist determination and commercial acumen had achieved political independence for a society and economy primarily shaped for economic efficiency. Thus far the liberators could see. What they could not see was the ensuing phase, when the independent Republic had to assume the burdens of its own defence against new enemies. First England and then France replaced Spain as the threat to Dutch liberty.

To fight in one's own defence may have been politically more satisfying than to owe helpless allegiance to a dynastic overlord. It was not less expensive. Try as they might to avoid war by the dogged pursuit of neutrality, by devious diplomacy, by the development of legal devices which enabled them to trade with combatants in war time, the Dutch could not wholly escape either its violence or its economic consequences. The Republic was only saved from annihilation in the French War of 1672–8 by a successful but economically devastating policy of flooding the countryside. Ineluctably the costs of defence at sea and in the Indies and elsewhere rose. There was a fatal contradiction between the basic search for normality, peace, and profit, and the ugly realities of the power politics of these centuries. The rebels of 1567 had been right to foresee the economic consequences of Alba and the Tenth Penny. Politically and morally the quest for independence might be noble, its achievement glorious; alas! its costs were stupendous.

The growing competition of rising economies like England and France and the increasing burden of taxes and costs was reflected in the absolute decline of former great centres of industry. By the mid eighteenth century, Leyden was a desolate town, its once flourishing cloth industry reduced to a fraction of its former size. The Haarlem linen industry was similarly shrunken. The decline of such industries can be traced in detail in surviving letters between Exeter and Topsham merchants and their Amsterdam correspondents. This branch of Anglo-Dutch trade had been based on an exchange of English cloth against Dutch linens, clover seed, hemp, sail cloth. About 1700 the English begin to complain of the costs and quality of Dutch goods. They can import them more cheaply, they write, from elsewhere. Scotland and Ireland are beginning to make finer linens than Haarlem. They can buy better hemp from Hamburg, Bremen or even Russia. They prefer to sell their cloth direct to Bilbao or Italy rather than pay a Dutch commission agent's fee.

Evidently the whole indirect trade which Holland had held for more than a century in her capacity as middleman was breaking down. Direct trade routes and direct connections between European producers and consumers, buyers and sellers were beginning to replace the entrepôt system based on Amsterdam. In terms of the profits of individual Dutch merchants, this meant more work for smaller returns. Hence a change in investment policy. If active trading and manufacturing were less attractive, finance and banking (in the broad sense) were more so. Too little is known about the activities of individual merchants for us to be sure whether and on what scale men who had previously manufactured products or actively bought and sold them actually withdrew their capital to become *rentiers*. But there is enough evidence to suggest that this happened on a sizeable scale. New men coming into business were attracted by the higher yields and easier life offered by finance as compared with the cut-throat competition in shipping, trade or industry. Why struggle to earn three per cent on your capital in trade when you could make five per cent or more by investing it in a loan to Prussia or Russia or the Emperor or the English?

Trading methods had long accustomed the Dutch merchants to the idea of advancing money in the form of credits to those who bought from them or sold to them. It was characteristic of the eighteenth century that banking and finance houses now sprang up whose business was increasingly to lend money to foreign governments. Houses like the Pels, Deutz, Cliffords, Neufvilles and many others borrowed savings from hundreds of institutions – almshouses, schools, guilds – and individuals and re-lent them to nearly every government in Europe.

These changes to a more specifically *rentier* economy were mirrored in changes in the Dutch colonies in Europe. They had originated as trading 'factories'. Now they became financiers and bankers. Ever since the Reformation, the great church of Austin Friars had been the communal centre of the Dutch in England. The Dutch Calvinist refugee community in London contributed much to the development of their Church in Holland. Here they had sung the first Dutch psalms in rhyme and proclaimed the first declarations of faith in Dutch. There was never a community (wrote Utenhove, one of the earliest of the Austin Friars elders) of such purity, sincerity and fidelity. When Alba's victims flooded in, in the 1560s, they had thankfully informed the Queen:

We live (God be thanked) under your Maiesties protection and safe-guarde in great libertie to serve God in either language, the Frenche or the Dutche, without al feare of tyrantes.

By the time of the South Sea Bubble in 1720 Austin Friars had taken on a different aspect. The great church was still (as its rebuilt successor is today) the centre of the Dutch community in Britain. But its elders and deacons were now great figures in the City. By the mid-century, Dutch London bankers like Sir Matthew Decker, the Van Neck brothers, the Crayesteyn brothers and a dozen others were financing private business and government on a tremendous scale. Their private fortunes were as large as any in the City. They lived sumptuously in great houses at Putney and Fulham with spacious lawns and gardens that ran down to the Thames. Others had splendid country estates where they dined, hunted and

inter-married with the country gentry. Joshua van Neck, who him-
self became a baronet and whose son joined the English peerage as
Lord Huntingfield, could underwrite a government loan in the
Seven Years War for over a million pounds.

These great operators were closely associated with the Bank of
England, the East India Company, the South Sea Company and
the world of insurance. (The first chairman of Lloyds was a Dutch
banker, Martin Kuyck van Mierop.) Their services were indispensable to successive Whig administrations. When the Tories
excoriated Whig methods as 'Dutch Finance', they were not far
wrong. For was not the Bank of England itself floated with Dutch
capital? And were not the Dutch bankers still amongst its largest
stockholders and customers in the 1760s? Through their offices,
the British were able to tap the savings of Dutch investors large and
small, of municipal almshouses and orphanages as well as of
private persons. The Van Neck network operated widely. They and
others of the Austin Friars Dutch colony were closely interwoven
by marriage, money and partnership with Huguenot families who
arrived in England after the revocation of the Edict of Nantes in
1685. These connections linked them in turn with rich and influential members of the so-called 'Banque Protestante', that network of banking dynasties that operated from France and Geneva
and throughout Europe. Thus was Dutch money funnelled into
England and, into Europe to pay for the maintenance of British
troops. Neutral observers put it high amongst the advantages
which England enjoyed in the wars of the eighteenth century.

London's other social centre for merchants in the Anglo-Dutch
trade and finance was the Sephardic Synagogue at Bevis Marks in
the City. This was a copy of the great synagogue at Amsterdam,
whence came many of its members – the De Pintos, Du Costas, De
Suassos etc. They operated on a smaller scale than the Christians of
Austin Friars but they included a few really important financiers,

London y⁵ Day of Jan¹¹ 1730/31

South Sea Stock	103	7/8 a 4
Ditto Annuities	106	3/8
India Stock	190	2
Bank Stock	143	7/8
Million Bank	108	
Lottery Annuities 3 ⅌ C^t	9/7	8/8
London Assurance	12	3/8
Royal Ditto	9/6	3/4
York Buildings Stock	27	1/4
African Stock	49	8/4
South Sea Bonds	£ 5ˢ 10
India Ditto	5ˢ 13

Refusals

	Gui. ⅌ C^t	⅌ C^t
India for 6/m^ths		
Ditto for 3/m		
South Sea for 6/m		
Ditto for 3/m		
Bank for 6/m		
Ditto for 3/m		

Putts

India for 6/m		
Ditto for 3/m		
South Sea for 6/m		
Ditto for 3/m		
Bank for 6/m		
Ditto for 3/m		

N° 8

Yo^r Most Obedient Servant

Stephen Daubuz

like Joseph Salvadore who was closely involved in Indian affairs and acted as adviser to Clive.

Nor were the London Dutch content with mere investment. A hundred or two yards from Austin Friars and Joshua van Neck's house and counting house in New Bond Street was Change Alley. Here, at Jonathan's Coffee House, Dutch speculators helped to reproduce the intricate apparatus of speculation which had already been perfected at Amsterdam a hundred years before: settlement or contango day, puts and calls, continuations, backwardation and all the refinements of the modern stock exchange came into action. The London Stock Exchange was the child of the Amsterdam parent. The two markets were linked by packet boats, like the *Eagle*, a boat of seventy tons that plied twice a week between Harwich and Helvoetsluys. On board the *Eagle* and its sister boats were the mails carrying news of the war or peace that would send the price of government stocks or of commodities up or down. Thus were great fortunes and spectacular bankruptcies made.

Not only the national debt itself, which was to be an increasingly formative force in the eighteenth-century economy in Britain, but the method of raising the interest on it, were powerfully influenced by Dutch practice. The 'excise', a convenient form of indirect taxation, was increasingly used by eighteenth-century governments: the system, and the name, were copied from the Dutch. The word itself was a corruption of the Dutch *accijns*. The proportion of the debt itself owned by the Dutch is almost impossible to calculate: but certainly English statesmen like Walpole, Newcastle and Lord North all recognised that Dutch support was indispensable to the public credit in London. So, on a smaller scale, did the French kings, Frederick the Great, Catherine the Great, the Emperor and a host of smaller princes in Scandinavia, Italy, Spain and central Europe.

Earlier chapters have touched on the way in which the Dutch example stimulated seventeenth-century English economic thinkers to try and emulate the results (which the Dutch had achieved by the spontaneous operation of enterprise) by means of state action. Just as the Dutch influenced in this way 'mercantilist' (*dirigiste*) ideas and policies in Europe, thereby helping to contrive their own downfall, so they also later influenced the growth of ideas of economic freedom. Adam Smith was popularly supposed to have been influenced in his ideas on the merits of free trade by the writings of Sir Matthew Decker who has been mentioned earlier. In an empirical way, Decker had stood out for freedom of trade, fewer and simpler taxes, and had attacked tariffs and monopolies. Perhaps some of this earthy, business-man's view of *laissez-faire* is embodied in *Wealth of Nations* (1776).

Adam Smith himself still praised the virtues of the Dutch, their serious attention to business, and the digression in which he explained the merits of the Bank of Amsterdam is still a classic piece of economic exposition. If he criticised their absurd indirect taxation (which he claimed compelled a man to buy a licence to drink a cup of tea), he admitted that it was the virtually inevitable result of wars into which Holland had been drawn unwillingly.

Even while he wrote, nemesis was fast approaching. England's wars with the American colonists and with France shook Dutch confidence in English credit. Dutch investors withdrew money from England and invested it in French and American securities. Holland was drawn into the Third English War in the 1780s. Both decisions proved disastrous. Large sums of money were lost and the Battle of Camperdown (1797) ended for the time being the long and glorious phase of Dutch sea power.

By the nineteenth century, Dutch trade and finance had been dwarfed by the scale of British industrial production, and the Dutch economy was only slowly and painfully adjusted to changed conditions. Even in Dickens's London, however, traces and traditions of the former wealth of the Dutch colony remained. In Dickens's *Christmas Carol* Scrooge sat and shivered over his gruel by a fireplace 'built by some Dutch merchant long ago, and paved all round with quaint Dutch tiles designed to illustrate the Scriptures.' Dickens may well have drawn upon real life for his fantasy; Scrooge's house could have been the home of the Van Necks, Van Hemerts or the eighteenth-century Dutch miser Crayesteyn, for Charles Dickens knew the City and its history: perhaps somewhere up by Austin Friars or New Broad Street, Scrooge's Delft tiles may still depict their

Cains and Abels, Pharaoh's daughters, Queens of Sheba, Angelic messengers descending through the air on clouds like feather beds, Abrahams, Belshazzars, Apostles putting off to sea in butter-boats . . .[44]

The phenomena of cultural decline in nations are infinitely absorbing: yet they have been little studied in any scientific sense. By 1750 the Dutch Republic had passed from the stage politically. Economically it was in a state of decline. All creative or innovatory power seemed to have been lost. The wealth of its *rentier* and financial society, and the power its money still exercised in the chancelleries of Europe, could not disguise its real poverty – that it was no longer forging new patterns of trade or introducing new products and technologies as it had done a century before. The history of the Dutch Republic had been the story of a people heaving themselves up by their own bootstraps with unbelievable determination. Now they seemed exhausted, physically and spiritually, perhaps by the long wars, by the knowledge that they were too small for their effort to count for much in the European struggle for power.

The physical, measurable evidence of decline was accompanied by a cultural *malaise*. There are few great Dutch names in the visual or social arts after the 1670s. Even in the Dutch galleries and museums the visitors will search in vain for any Dutch artists of the eighteenth century to compare with Vermeer, Cuyp or Ruysdael. The one likely starter, Cornelius Troost, a dramatic and satirical artist of great merit, is still little known outside Holland, and it is significant, if unfair, that Troost has often been regarded as either a secondary Hogarth or a derivative from the French classical tradition. But the thought was characteristic – the stream of ideas and influences was now reversed, in the arts as in science, technology and trade. There was to be a long, dull and painful period of revaluation before a new culture could arise.

Yet the world could be thankful for the qualities of life and thought which the Dutch had transmitted to it between the rise of the Dutch Republic and its fall two centuries later. They were the first people to break the hold of political dynasticism by deliberate rebellion. In economic life they had broken the tyranny of custom, substituting rational and scientific method for ingrained habit. In art they had developed a new *genre*, secular and realistic, in place of the devotional art of the later Middle Ages. To science they had brought a belief in precision and a determination to root out inaccuracy and superstition. In a century of political and religious bigotry they cultivated a sense of freedom none the worse for being grounded in self-interest, and united in rare marriage with a passion for good order. To painting they brought an eye for detail, a naturalism that illuminated the simple theme by brilliant observation. To philosophy, a faith in free thought and reasonableness that shunned flamboyance and exaggeration.

These might be northern virtues; they could become dull, unimaginative, pedestrian. But at best they could distil into purest wisdom and sheer beauty. This was the cultural legacy of the Dutch Republic to Europe and the world. Its impact has been felt everywhere in Europe, but most of all in what may be called the

'North Sea Economy' – Scandinavia, north Germany, north France and England. Anglo-Dutch economic rivalry itself had contributed powerfully to transform England from a feudal to a modern society. The Dutch had also helped to transmit to northern Europe much that was culturally Mediterranean in art, architecture, medicine, mathematics and philosophy. Defoe had described them as 'the factors and brokers of Europe'; but they were the middlemen of culture as well as of trade. In the course of meeting the challenge of their situation – the inherent poverty that drove them to create a landscape with shovels and an economy with fishing nets – they had developed a society with its own unique and unmistakable characteristics. These in turn had powerfully affected neighbouring states.

Much in the civilisation of the seventeenth century can only be understood in the light of the Dutch Revolt and the society that grew up in its wake. Very much larger nations, France and England especially, were to exercise more influence on the political institutions and the patterns of power in the world than the small Dutch Republic could possibly wield. But where the material arts and sciences, the visual and social arts, and concepts of social welfare and intellectual freedom were concerned, the Dutch could claim at least an equal influence. Without their creative energies, the civilisation of the seventeenth century as we know it could not have existed.

GENERAL: the most recent comprehensive survey of Netherlands history is the *Algemene Geschiedenis der Nederlanden* by a team of eminent Netherlands historians, in 12 volumes (Utrecht 1949–58). For those who do not read Dutch, the best survey will be found in Professor P. Geyl's *Revolt of the Netherlands* (5th edition 1966) and *The Netherlands in the Seventeenth Century* Parts 1 and 2 (1961 and 1963). These form part of his great work, *Geschiedenis Van de Nederlandse Stam* (Amsterdam 1930–37).

BIOGRAPHICAL AND POLITICAL: the most understanding study of *Erasmus* is that by the great Dutch historian J. Huizinga (Haarlam 1924). There are also English versions (New York 1924: London 1952). F. Rachfahl's *Wilhelm von Oranien und der Niederländische Aufstand* (Halle and The Hague 1907) though in some respects old-fashioned is still valuable. C. V. Wedgwood's *William the Silent* (1944) is the most readable biography of William. The most convenient commentary on Grotius is still W. S. Knight's *Life and Works of Hugo Grotius* (1925).

ECONOMIC: Violet Barbour's *Capitalism of Amsterdam in the Seventeenth Century* (Baltimore 1950) gives a valuable conspectus of Dutch economic influence in Europe. D. W. Davies's *A Primer of Dutch Overseas Trade* (The Hague 1961), though making no attempt at analysis, contains much vivid factual information. The best recent account of Netherlands economic and social history is by Professor J. A. Van Houtte, *Economische en Sociale Geschiedenis Van de Lage Landen* (Zeist and Antwerp, 1964). For the phase of change and decline see C. Wilson *Anglo-Dutch Commerce and Finance in the Eighteenth Century* (2nd Edition 1966) and the same author's essay on *The Decline of the Netherlands*, reprinted in *Essays in Economic History* edited by E. Carus-Wilson (1954). A thorough if unexciting survey of Dutch economic development is provided by E. Baasch, *Holländische Wirtschaftsgeschichte* (Jena 1927). Striking evidence of Dutch economic penetration of Scandinavia will be found in E. Heckscher's *Sveriges Ekonomiska Historia* (Stockholm 1935), an English version of which appeared an *An Economic History of Sweden* (Cambridge, Mass. 1954). The enterprise of individual Dutch merchants in Sweden and elsewhere can be found in P. W. Klein's *De Trippen in de 17ᵉ Eeuw* (Assen 1965).

A synopsis of this study by the author may be found in English in *Acta Historiae Neerlandica* (Leiden 1967). A. B. van Veen traces the history of a rival Dutch concern in Scandinavia in his *Louis de Geer* (Amsterdam 1935). F. Braudel's *La Mediterranée* (Paris 1949) explores evidence of Dutch economic enterprise in Italian and Mediterranean trade and industry. J. Korthals Altes reviews Dutch attempts to drain the Roman marshes in Vol. VI of the *Mededelingen Ned. Hist. Inst. te Rome*. H. Heaton's *Economic History of Europe* (New York 1948) contains useful information on the Dutch world economy. Sir George Clark's *Seventeenth Century* (1947) contains many original ideas on the Dutch in their economic, as in most other aspects. For Dutch influence on French trades and industry, see G. Martin's *La Grande Industrie sous le règne de Louis XIV* (Paris 1889). W. Cunningham's *Alien Immigrants to England* (1897) remains the best survey of Dutch immigration into Britain.

SOCIAL DEVELOPMENT: Paul Zumthor's *La Vie Quotidienne en Hollande au temps de Rembrandt* (Paris 1960) contains much concrete evidence and many apposite illustrations of Dutch social life. It appeared in English in 1962 as *Daily Life in Rembrandt's Holland*. G. Renier's *The Dutch Nation* (1944) is a discursive but always stimulating account of the nature of Dutch society. On the regent class, one of the best recent comments is the essay P. Geyl printed in his *History of the Low Countries* (Trevelyan Lectures 1964). Rachfahl's work mentioned earlier is still useful on the activities of the nobility, major and minor. *De Vroedschap Van Amsterdam* by J. E. Elias (Haarlem 1903–05) is a study of the important families of Amsterdam, uniquely detailed and extensive.

PEACE AND WAR: on Grotius and the development of international law, T. W. Fulton's *Sovereignty of the Seas* (1911) though now over half a century old is still indispensable. The economic frictions behind the wars are dealt with in C. Wilson's *Profit and Power* (1958).

ART: the best general survey is that by Professor H. E. van Gelder in his *Guide to Dutch Art* (The Hague 1961). Paul Zumthor's study mentioned earlier has interesting material on the social background to the artists' life.

Arnold Hauser has suggestive interpretations to offer in his *Sozialgeschichte der Kunst und Literatur* (Munich 1953). The English version is *A Social History of Art* (1951). Sir J. Rothenstein's *Introduction to English Painting* (1933) shows how England's debt to Dutch artists arose. A. W. von Wurzbach's *Niederländisches Künstler Lexikon* (Leipzig and Vienna 1906–11) will be valuable for reference. But the best sources here are the paintings, drawings and buildings themselves, spread widely throughout Europe and America.

LITERATURE: excellent work has been done in recent years at the Thomas Browne Institute at Leiden University on Dutch cultural relations with Britain and Europe. Professor A. G. H. Bachrach (the director) has contributed a fascinating study of *Sir Constantine Huyghens and Britain* (Leiden 1962). Dr. J. A. Van Dorsten explores other cultural connections in his *Poets, Patrons and Professors* (Leiden 1962). The influence of Addison and Steele in Holland is examined in W. J. Pienaar's *English Influences in Dutch Literature and Justus van Effen as Intermediary* (1929). The Milton-Vondel controversy may be studied in Edmund Gosse's *Studies in the Literature of Northern Europe* (1879) and in G. Edmundson's *Milton and Vondel* (1885).

SCIENCE AND TECHNOLOGY: Sir George Clark's *Science and Social Welfare in the Age of Newton* (1937) is valuable. Professor E. G. R. Taylor's *The Haven Finding Art* (1956) links Dutch and English navigational advance. Clifford Dobell's delightful edition of *Antony van Leeuwenhoek and his Little Animals* (1932) gives a first-hand view of the scientist's work.

PHILOSOPHY: Spinoza's works can best be studied in A. G. Wernham's Oxford edition of 1958. The best brief survey of the philosophers referred to is in G. N. Clark's *Seventeenth Century*.

SCOTLAND: religious connections with Holland are examined in G. D. Henderson's *Religious Life in Seventeenth Century Scotland* (1936). Economic connections are the subject of *The Scottish Staple at Veere* (The Hague 1910) a work by a Dutch scholar (M. P. Rooseboom) but written in English. The unique annals of The Scots Brigade in Holland were set out by James Ferguson in 3 volumes (Scottish Historical Society 1899).

COLONIES: the best and most recent survey is Professor C.R.Boxer's *The Dutch Seaborne Empire 1600–1800* (New York and London 1965).

HISTORIOGRAPHY, ETC.: the two volumes of papers of the conferences of Anglo-Dutch historians published under the title *Britain and the Netherlands* (Vol. I 1960: Vol. II Groningen 1964) contain much valuable reading on a variety of topics concerning Dutch life and history (edited by J.Bromley and E.J.Kossmann).

Many of the works quoted above (e.g. Geyl, Barbour, Boxer, Davies, Wilson) contain more detailed bibliographies for readers who wish to carry their enquiries further, including works in Dutch, French and German as well as English.

Notes

1 Quoted by J. Huizinga *Erasmus of Rotterdam* (London and New York, 1952) p.229. Translated from *Opus Epistolarum Des. Erasmi Roterodami* (Oxford, 1906–47.) ed P.S. and H.M. Allen. Letter to Beatus Rhenanus *c*.15 October 1518. Vol. III No. 867.

2 Quoted by Huizinga *op. cit.* p. 232. Original in Allen. Letter to Ulrich Hutten 23 July 1519. Vol. IV. No. 999.

3 Huizinga *op. cit.* p. 165. From *Hyperaspistes* (1526).

4 Huizinga *op. cit.* p. 194.

5 Deventer *Gedenkstukken* Vol. II, 290–3.

6 Daniel Defoe *A Plan of the English Commerce* (1728) p. 192.

7 Andrew Marvell *Character of Holland* (1653)

8 Descartes *Oeuvres* ed. Adam and Tannery Vol. I, p. 203. Quoted in Gustave Cohen *Ecrivains Français en Hollande* (Paris, 1920) p. 464.

9 Gustav Renier *The Dutch Nation* (1944) p. 105: quoting L. Aitzema *Saken Van Staet en Oorlogh* (1669–71)

10 Gustav Renier *op. cit.* p. 23.

11 J. de Witt *The True Interest and Political Maxims of the Republick of Holland* (English Edition of 1702) p. 242.

12 Grotius *The Freedom of the Seas* ed. J. B. Scott (New York and Oxford, 1916) p. 4. Subsequent quotations from Grotius are taken from this source.

13 John Selden *Of the Dominion or Ownership of the Sea* (translated from the Latin by Marchamont Needham 1652); Author's Preface p. (f).

14 Boswell's Life of Johnson (Oxford, 1957) p. 321.

15 Boswell *op. cit.* p. 815.

16 Huet *Mémoires* quoted by V. Barbour *Capitalism in Amsterdam in the Seventeenth Century* (Baltimore, 1950) p. 118.

17 J. Savary *Le Parfait Négociant* (1675) quoted Barbour *op. cit.* p. 118.

18 Samuel Smiles *James Brindley and the Early Engineers* (1864) p. 36.

19 Ibid.

20 Quoted by Lord Ernle *English Farming Past and Present* (1961) p. 138.

21 E. Wright *Certaine Errores of Navigation* (1599).

22 C. Huygens *Opera Varia* (1724) Biographical Introduction.

23 *Gentleman's Magazine* (1738) Obituary of Boerhaave.

24 William Shakespeare *Twelfth Night* III, 2.

25 *Social History of Art* (1951) Vol I. p. 462.

26 Paul Zumthor *Everyday Life in Rembrandt's Holland* (p. 198).

27 Samuel Pepys *Diary* (ed. Rhys 1943) Vol. II. p. 28.

28 Matthew Prior *The Conversation* (1720). *Collected Poems* (1863).

29 Fynes Moryson's *Itinerary* quoted in A.G.H.Bachrach *Sir Constantine Huyghens and Britain* (1962) p. 96.

30 *Spectator* No. 10.

31 W.J.Pienaar *English Influences in Dutch Literature* p. 180 and Ch. V *passim* (1930).

32 B.de Spinoza in the *Tractatus Theologico-Politicus* (*1670*) printed in *The Political Works* ed. A.G.Wernham (1958) p. 241.

33 G.N.Clark *The Seventeenth Century* (1947) p. 260.

34 R.Colie in *Britain and the Netherlands* (ed. Bromley and Kossmann 1959) p. 129.

35 E.Kossmann in *Britain and the Netherlands* p. 105.

36 *Letters and Papers relating to the First Dutch War 1652–4* (Navy Records Society ed. Gardiner and Atkinson 1898–1930) Vol. I Part I. No. 2.

37 Pepys *Diary*. 16 November, 1665. (Rhys Edition p. 653).

38 Quoted by C.R.Boxer *The Dutch Seaborne Empire* (London and New York, 1965) p. 96.

39 *Documents Relative to the Colonial History of the State of New York* ed. J.R.Brodhead (New York, 1856) Vol. I. p. 264.

40 J.E.Heeres *The Part Borne by the Dutch in the Discovery of Australia 1606–1765* (1899) p. 4.

41 Quoted by Boxer *op. cit.* p. 50.

42 *Ibid.* p. 231–2.

43 Printed in *The Clarke Papers* Vol III ed. C.H.Firth (1899) p. 175.

44 Charles Dickens *A Christmas Carol* (1843)

Acknowledgments

Acknowledgment – further to any made in the captions – is due to the following for illustrations (the number refers to the page on which the illustration appears). 9,28–9,105, 226 (*below*) Radio Times Hulton Picture Library; 24, 238, Author; 26, Topografische Atlas Gem. Archiefdienst, Amsterdam; 38, 54, 98, 216, Mansell Collection; 53, 97, A. Dingjan, Den Haag; 70, Archives du Ministère des Affaires Etrangères, Paris (photo: Service International de Microfilm); 77, Colchester and Essex Museum (photo: Brian Philp); 78–9, Het Nederlands Instituut te Rome; 85, Corporation of London; 94 (*right*) C.F.D.R.U. Leiden; 104, Ronan Picture Library and Royal Astronomical Society; 106 (*top*) University Museum, Utrecht and Dr J.G. van Cittert-Eymers; (*below*) Leeuwenhoek Commission (Dr J.J. Swart); 108, 126–7, 217, Rijkmuseum, Amsterdam; 122 The Marquess of Bute; 153 Instituut voor Neerlandistiek, Amsterdam; 158, 174, (*right*) Universiteitsbibliotheek, Amsterdam; 167, Ronan Picture Library and E.P. Goldschmidt; 179, W.L. den Beer Poortugael, Veere; 186–7 Kon. Penningkabinet, Den Haag; 225, Rembrandthuis Amsterdam; 226 (*top*) Tropenmuseum, Amsterdam 227;

The maps were drawn by Design Practitioners Limited. That on pages 80–1 is based on maps in *Dredge, Drain, Reclaim* by J. van Veen (Nijhoff, The Hague, 1962).

Index

254

World University Library

Already published